D0477288

ALBERT JOHN TASKER

INCHON

MacArthur's Last Triumph

GENERAL OF THE ARMY DOUGLAS MacARTHUR

INCHON

MacArthur's Last Triumph

Michael Langley

BATSFORD

First published 1979
© Michael Langley 1979

All rights reserved. No part of this publication
may be reproduced in any form or by any means
without permission from the Publishers.

ISBN 0-7134-3346-9

Printed in the U.S.A.
for the publishers, B. T. Batsford Ltd
4 Fitzhardinge Street, London W1H OAH

Dedicated to the memory of
GENERAL OF THE ARMY DOUGLAS MACARTHUR,
and to the alliance of the United Nations
in a just cause.

Hoc volo, sic jubeo, sit pro ratione voluntas.
Juvenal; *Satires,* vi, 223.

Acknowledgments

I am greatly indebted to Colonel Heinl for his encouragement and advice; but, as I explain in Appendix C, our purposes were not identical. Otherwise, my thanks are owed to my agent, Mr. David Bolt of Bolt and Watson Limited, and to my publishers, B. T. Batsford Limited, who, owing to a misfortune, accepted my completed manuscript three days late. I am grateful notably to Mr. Bill Waller, the Editorial Director, who negotiated the manuscript and was fortunate to find for us so reputable a publisher in the United States as Times Books. I am also very pleased to see that my book is to be published by Fitzhenry & Whiteside, Ltd., of Toronto, ever conscious of the invaluable contribution which Canada made to the Commonwealth Division during the Korean War.

Contents

List of Maps

Introduction

The Korean campaign is complicated when being retold to the public at large because, like World War II (but without the popular history which has informed younger generations of its main details) one must write for the well-informed (even for veterans) and for the totally ignorant to whom one must try to "sell" the subject. Some of my readers may have served under General MacArthur in the Pacific and/or Korea, and others may only know of his name. To many of us the latter sounds incredible, but then which of us is fully conversant with the life of, say, Lord Kitchener? They were military proconsuls of the same stature. I hope that I have satisfied all who wish to know a little more about the last great amphibious landing in history, be they groups of readers covering a gap of years which yawns as widely as did that between Inchon and Pusan. But to the military historian, no less than to the cursory dabbler, the closing of that was a miracle worthy of Cannae, Xerxes at the Hellespont, or Dunkirk. But of that I have plenty to say.

This book, I confidently believe, is the first separate study of the campaign to be written by an Englishman. I have treated it strategically as the great fulcrum of the Korean War, diplomatically as the offensive that nearly left America to pursue the war alone, and revolutionarily as the campaign that made limited war a necessity; and, naturally, I have followed the course of the fortnight over every mile of the advance from Inchon to the breakout from Seoul, so that I have tried at least to indicate every dimension of this vital part of a war which, for some strange reason, is already passing into military oblivion. The United States, of course, dominated the strength of the allies, but it is suitable that an Englishman should at last write of Inchon because the Korean War was the first in which the assailants were collectively checked by the express wish of the United Nations, their opponents throughout; and at Inchon, no less, Britain (whose armies were fully occupied all over the world) contributed a naval force. Even in the United States I do not believe that there are more than two accounts of the Inchon-Seoul offensive—the *Official History of the Marine Corps in the Korean War* (volume 2) and that of Colonel Robert D. Heinl, Jr., in which, so he claimed to me, he was able to use more up-to-date statistics. The latter work, a fine book, was republished in London in 1972.

From the flotsam of war the tragic twilight battles of the Korean War deserve better than simply to be forgotten by a succeeding generation of less vigilant and more fearful assembly of United Nations. Korea was the last of the old wars, when there were victors and vanquished, and the first of the new, when the indigenous people were alleged to decide the point with their feet. And Inchon, itself, was the fulcrum of Korea, which insured the prevalence of sanity in the arsenals of the West.

Michael Langley

January 1, 1979

INCHON

MacArthur's
Last Triumph

CHAPTER ONE

The Old General
and the Korean War

The possession of Korea has been disputed many times; this book is essentially concerned not with the most recent war to be waged up and down the length of the peninsula, but with that battle which became the most strategic landmark of the conflict—Inchon, the last great amphibious operation in history. In purely military terms it was Quebec, Maida, Normandy, and Lingayen worked to perfection. Yet a great commander of flair and genius, who would have impressed himself upon the military situation of any age, was relieved of his command, and the war—the last orthodox and first limited war in modern history—could produce neither victor nor vanquished. The uneasy armistice, negotiated along the positions held on July 27, 1953 (almost on what was called "Line Kansas"), has been broken numerous times by the communists, never more severely than during the summer of 1976 when American troops of the U.N. were shot by border guards because they were cutting down some apple trees allegedly in North Korea. It was a portentious incident.

The United Nations' resistance to the North Korean invasion on June 24, 1950, prevented the rape of the entire peninsula by the communists, but it purported to find no ultimate solution to the Korean problem. Inchon was monstrously daring, but it would be the last occasion when communist powers would watch their enemy carry the field quite so convincingly. However they would try to dictate the enemy's strategy or tactics in future, Inchon was too impressive a spectacle—and far too

3

much of an embarrassment for the Sino-Soviet axis—to offer a watching world. Whether or not MacArthur was too headstrong will be discussed, but certainly it was by an unhappy sequence of events that the General led the allies back to the frontier and then, with whatever justification he felt he had, decided that he should not halt his advance until he had reached the Yalu River bordering Manchuria.

The brief Inchon–Seoul offensive, removed from the context of the disasters which preceded and succeeded it, was a peerless operation, although it is invidious to make comparisions where there are so many disparate factors. But Inchon possessed and fully utilized those two precious ingredients, skill and luck; and if, at any time, the latter was lacking, the former maximized it to whatever capacity was required in the achievement of subsequent tasks. The invasion from the sea opened a second front in Korea and, but for the invasion of Chinese "volunteers," would have concluded the war in a few weeks.

The maverick character of the Korean War came as a surprise to those who thought of wars as conflicts requiring the decencies of declaration, preferably from a pre-arranged hour in the Chamberlain manner. These decencies should still have been observed even where the weapons were fiendish. The Spanish Civil War, when anyone could play uninvited, was essentially civil strife, internationally exploited. But when the Chinese "volunteers" entered the fray in Korea and reversed the situation created by the speed and brilliance of MacArthur's assault on Inchon (known militarily as *Operation Chromite*), the customary nature of warfare—with the notorious exception of Pearl Harbor—changed with it.

The Inchon–Seoul offensive ushered in the age of the limited war. Historically, it was the fulcrum of military strategy where, to minimize the danger of atomic warfare, hostilities would exist only on or in the vicinity of the disputed territory. Military philosophers invoked von Clausewitz to help them redefine war and peace as favorably as smooth relations would allow, although Gen. MacArthur held firm to the belief that victory or defeat was the only logical conclusion to war. But henceforth wars would become fought vicariously on sordid street corners. They would be without the customary chivalry and with little honor. Korea was the last conflict to witness both military beliefs, the conventional war and the war that contained hostilities at any price *in loco belli*. The British Battle of the Hook, one of the last in Korea, marked the end of the set-piece engagements; but if one were to invoke the great battles of history then the Inchon–Seoul offensive, which like the second Battle of El Alamein lasted about a fortnight, by the genius and precision of its planning and execution in the face of a plethora of natural and human hazards, must rank with Xerxes' bridging of the Hellespont, with Wolfe's landing at Quebec and—most closely—with Cannae because the brilliance of its conduct, like Hannibal's, was followed eventually by the ignominy of retreat.

But MacArthur must remain one of a small but gallant corps of modern commanders of whom it could be said, as H.A.L. Fisher wrote of Napoleon:

He remains the great modern example of that reckless and defiant insolence which formed the matter of human tragedy and is at war with the harmonies of human life.[1]

It is essential to place Inchon in the context of the Korean War as a whole because, however brilliant a feat of arms and deserving of individual attention, it was, as I have said, the fulcrum on which the whole military and diplomatic conduct of the war balanced. Its outstanding and unexpected success allegedly inspired the first surreptitious movement southward of the Chinese "volunteers," masterminded by the Army commander, Marshal Lin Piao (who vanished in mysterious circumstances in about 1971), and commanded by Gen. Peng Te-huai, when the essential communist initiative passed from Russia to China and so to what MacArthur called "an entirely new war." That the Commander in Chief, by training, bias, and long experience, should himself have led the United Nations forces at this moment in such a development and departure from orthodoxy (for even such a maverick as he was orthodox) was a notable irony of military history; for while he was best able to carry the Inchon–Seoul offensive, he was least able to adapt himself to the strategy which the enemy's unexpected as-

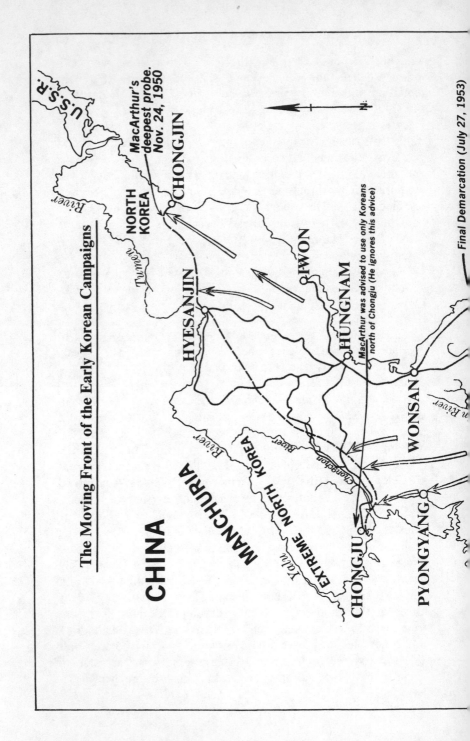

The Moving Front of the Early Korean Campaigns

CHINA

MANCHURIA

U.S.S.R.

River

Tumen River

NORTH KOREA

CHONGJIN

MacArthur's deepest probe. Nov. 24, 1950

HYESANJIN

IWON

HUNGNAM

MacArthur was advised to use only Koreans north of Chongju (He ignores this advice)

EXTREME NORTH KOREA

Yalu River

Chongchon River

WONSAN

CHONGJU

PYONGYANG

River

N.

Final Demarcation (July 27, 1953)

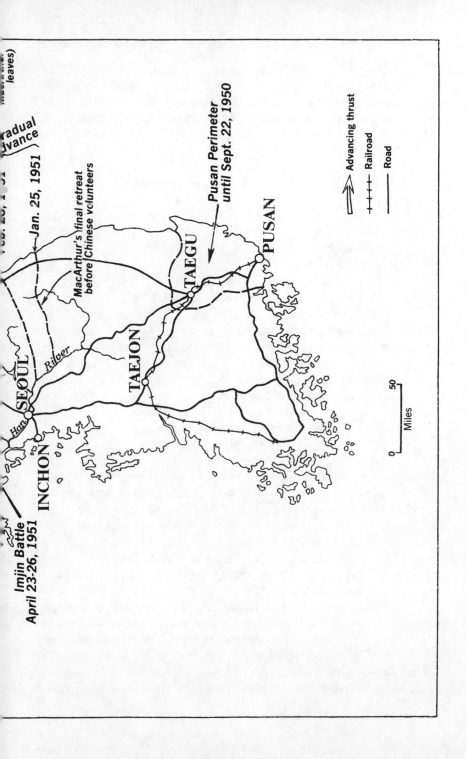

Imjin Battle
April 23-26, 1951

INCHON

SEOUL

Han.

Ri/ver

Jan. 25, 1951

MacArthur's final retreat
before Chinese volunteers

TAEJON

TAEGU

Pusan Perimeter
until Sept. 22, 1950

PUSAN

0   50
Miles

Advancing thrust
Railroad
Road

sault would require. This chapter, therefore, is devoted to Gen. MacArthur in the context of the Korean War and to a military assessment of the war in general, from which the full significance of the remarkable Inchon landing may be gauged. To treat Inchon in isolation would be to distort its importance and deny to the reader the opportunity of judging its overall relationship with the rest of the war. And although the leaders of the democracies were concerned primarily with Europe, MacArthur agreed that Europe witnessed only a war with words; whereas if he lost the Korean War Europe would be jeopardized.

At 0400 hours local time on Sunday, June 25, 1950, the North Korean People's Army (hereafter referred to as the NKPA) invaded the Republic of Korea by crossing the 38th parallel. From that moment there followed what was, in some respects, the most critical conflict to have arisen since World War II, and perhaps the most precipitate conflict of modern times. It was the first and most overt undeclared war actually to be created in the atomic age, and one in which a superpower was, even at that early stage, directly involved, albeit under a unified command which was to be set up within a few days. The Russians, equally thinly veiled as the real impulse behind the invasion, had set off their first atomic device nine months earlier. The situation was extremely perilous, for methods of avoiding the ultimate weapon had not yet been tried during renewed active hostility in a war beyond Hiroshima and Nagasaki, and they were to have strange effects upon conventional warfare. Although local, it was fraught with such military and political danger, and the death toll was so heavy, that the Korean must rank as a major war.

From the western point of view it was the last to be waged in the anticipation of total victory and the first in which priority was given to holding the enemy on a prearranged line in an attempt at conciliation. From it arose the concept of the "limited war," not so much as a philosophical idea but as a necessity. The watershed between these two politico-military notions occurred in the spring of 1951 with the dismissal by President Truman of the Commander in Chief, United Nations Command, and unquestionably the world's most senior and experienced active soldier. That the President could so treat MacArthur required great moral courage by Truman in the face of what became almost a national crisis. For public consumption through the media the President was satisfied quite simply to say:

> With deep regret I have concluded that General of the Army Douglas MacArthur is unable to give his wholehearted support to the policies of the United States Government and of the United Nations in matters pertaining to his official duties. In view of these specific responsibilities imposed upon me by the Constitution of the United States and the added responsibility which has been entrusted to me by the United Nations, I have decided that I must make a change.[2]

He was later to admit quite frankly that he wondered why he had not made a change years before. He had reached his decision quite independently, but on seeking to satisfy his action found that he had the support of General of the Army George Marshall,* that venerable military figure who had been Chief of Staff of the U.S. Army during World War II (an appointment held by MacArthur between 1930 and 1935) and, in varying degrees, by each of the Joint Chiefs of Staff and their Chairman. Implicitly all these commanders had acknowledged for the Korean War the Clausewitzian dogma that war is "a continuation of political intercourse, a carrying out of the same by other means,"[3] a concept with which, as I shall illustrate, Mac-Arthur profoundly disagreed; in other words, von Clausewitz, that eminent military philosopher of post-Napoleonic Europe, believed that war should be waged only in a manner prescribed by its limited political objectives.

The amphibious landing at Inchon on September 15, 1950, was, apart from the smaller assault at Iwon by the 7th Infantry Division on October 29th, the last operation of its kind—and second only to Normandy in scale—in the tradition of Quebec, Maida, East Africa in 1914, Gallipoli, North Africa (*Operation*

---

* We know from Alanbrooke's Diaries that Marshall lived in daily dread during World War II of Churchill's unorthodoxy, such as the Dardanelles, and also, presumably, of MacArthur's. See Bryant, *The Turn of the Tide*, p. 684.

Torch), and the several which MacArthur had learned to perfect against the Japanese in the Pacific. Today it is unthinkable that such warfare could ever again be conducted on that scale. Inchon illustrated the ultimate in planning and execution, prepared with minimal warning when weight of weaponry tried to minimize this deficiency. Even before 1950, the Chairman of the Joint Chiefs of Staff, Gen. Omar Bradley, could not have foreseen Inchon when he declared on October 19, 1949, that "I also predict that large-scale amphibious operations . . . will never occur again." [4] Bradley had never cared for the Marines to whom he referred in public as "fancy Dans." His belief so impressed the Defense Secretary, Louis Johnson, that major cuts to the strength of the Navy and the Marine Corps were already in progress by the outbreak of the Korean War. This would have jeopardized *Chromite* altogether had MacArthur, by his reputation and pleading for Inchon, not managed to reverse the procedure. That factor will be studied later in this chapter, which will also question the common supposition that MacArthur's influence on the Korean War increased the chances of an atomic confrontation.

That the whole concept of military strategy had changed as a result of the Korean War was a fact which had still not been grasped by the architects of the Suez invasion which, however well planned by the British, French, and Israelis, I have excepted from my list. The war in Vietnam was essentially that of the politicians, because the consequences of misdirected military initiative would be so catastrophic to the future of civilization that politicians dared not delegate responsibility. President Truman had stated the degree of responsibility he placed upon Gen. MacArthur; and so, leaving aside all military considerations, here is an historical precedent that so evidently has its roots in the Korean War. The Vietnam War, although more expensive in lives and equipment and far more protracted, was potentially less explosive than its predecessor, and Korea witnessed the more determined and better disciplined conduct by the Americans; as witnessed by this order of the day, written in Korea by Gen. Walton H. Walker, commander of the U.S. Eighth Army during its brave withdrawal to the Pusan perimeter where it produced such stoical resistance:

There will be no more retreating, withdrawal, readjustment of lines or whatever else you call it. There are no lines behind which we can retreat. This is not going to be a Dunkirk or Bataan. A retreat to Pusan would result in one of the greatest butcheries in history. We must fight until the end. We must fight as a team. If some of us must die, we will die fighting together.[5]

To the cynic these words would do for any histrionic Hollywood script, but in the heat of battle they do not flow so easily from a retreating commander. Walker was MacArthur's right-hand man at the start in Korea and one can almost hear the Commander in Chief's voice here. I doubt if any such stirring encouragement was given to the men in Vietnam, subverted by doubt and lack of faith in themselves, and lacking that integrity which was the hallmark of all forces who served with the United Nations Command. I do not wish to deviate, but it is worth commenting that the United States should have led a U.N. Command in Vietnam and Cambodia, as it had previously done, because communist China was anxious to be admitted to the General Assembly and would accordingly have restrained its desire to keep the Viet Cong so well supplied, with the shortening of the war which would have followed.

In the early fifties the American commanders in Korea were household names, even in Britain—Ridgway, Mark Clark, Van Fleet, the luckless C. Turner Joy who headed the allied delegation at the truce talks, and Maxwell Taylor (and not only because some had become known during World War II or because Britain had two brigades in the field); whereas the military commanders in Vietnam were obscure to most of us. There would certainly have been no room for MacArthur. One might picturesquely say that Korea saw the twilight of the military commander as a decisive force, personified by the patriotic old frontiersman of this chapter.

I shall discuss three aspects of the war before going ashore with *Operation Chromite*:

1. the causes and course of the campaign in which I hope to show Inchon to have been the crux of the war;

2. the character and background of the man who most

evidently changed the complexion of the military and diplomatic duel; and
3. the wider context of the war, incorporating a brief history, in terms of the omnipresent atomic threat which could, by 1950, be launched by the United States, Britain, and Russia.

Recent history had shaped and re-shaped Korea. While hostilities were eventually concluded with communist China, they had originally been inspired by Russia. To both had the North Koreans acted as stooge, particularly the latter whose campaigns they manned vicariously while allowing the Chinese to fight their own wars after their indistinguishable hordes had arrived from Manchuria. But here was a matter of territorial rather than ideological importance to Russia from whom Japan had seized Korea by conquest as a result of the 1904–06 war * and so held it for 40 years. The southern half, however, was not so easily raped by the Soviets. That attempt would have to wait for nearly five years, for perhaps the final putsch of Joseph Stalin in which the puppet North Koreans were entirely armed and encouraged by the wily old dictator. At the Cairo Conference of December, 1943, Britain, the United States, and China (represented by Gen. Chiang Kai-shek) agreed that after the defeat of Japan, Korea should become a free sovereign state. But then Imperial China had also been defeated by the Japanese in 1894-95 and, as with Russia, one can see their ulterior motive. The Cairo agreement was reaffirmed at Potsdam in June, 1945, on the eve of the Soviet Union's declaration of war on Japan which occurred on August 8th, timed to coincide with the atomic attacks on Hiroshima (August 6th) and Nagasaki (August 9th). From this mere gesture of hostility the Soviet Union emerged with considerable profit. Professing to adhere to the principles laid down at Cairo and Potsdam, it was entrusted with the surrender of Japanese forces north of the 38th parallel, while the United States would accept surrender to the south. Thus the Soviet Union was one step nearer to retrieving the situation which had existed before 1904, albeit then under a Czarist regime. But it was soon evident that

* Korea was formally annexed by Japan in 1910.

the communists regarded the parallel as a political frontier. Remembering the unjust and primitive old Roman law of *occupatio,* one realizes that international and constitutional progress, between objective and altruistic parties, can only be made in moments of self-denial when trust is supported by the maintenance of pledge, such as one might witness today in Israel's abandonment of the Golan Heights and Syria's not taking advantage of it. Short of such integrity, soldiers such as Douglas MacArthur will always be able to argue with conviction that promises are only kept by force of arms. But then, such men as MacArthur are a vanished species.

The situation in Korea continued to crystallize, and with it came the complete nullification of the benefits which had been created by Japanese industrialization, for the Korean iron curtain along the parallel was an arbitrary division which had no economic, social, or topographical foundation; although, generally speaking, the heavy industry was restricted to the north while the capital, Seoul, lay below the new frontier as did thousands of square miles of millet and rice paddy. As the divergence continued the two portions of Korea produced their own political and ideological leaders. And now South Korea is primarily industrial.

South Koreans could look at once to the father-figure and ageing patriot, Dr. Syngman Rhee, already elected President under the auspices of the United Nations. He had established a government-in-exile in Shanghai as far back as 1919, during the Japanese occupation. His overriding ambition, as the Americans were to discover to their severe embarrassment during the last stages of the armistice negotiations at Panmunjom in 1953, was the complete reunification of Korea as promised by the allies at Cairo and Potsdam; but now with communism officially outlawed. An autocrat who had fallen out of step with current thinking, he found some common purpose and understanding only with MacArthur and other like-minded commanders of traditional beliefs, such as Whitney, Doyle Hickey and Almond (who led X Corps at Inchon); but the intricacies of the limited war that followed MacArthur's recall, which had begun to be apparent during the early months of 1951, were completely beyond him. Leadership over the North was reposed in the person of Kim Il-sung (as it still is), who had been an active guerrilla leader during the Japanese occupation since the communists had first established resistance in 1935. Having also served the communist cause in Russia itself, where he is reputed to have fought at Stalingrad, he had returned to Korea in 1945 as a 35-year old major in the Soviet occupation forces.

From 1946, the Americans made every effort to implement the Potsdam Agreement, but were eventually obliged to refer the whole matter to the General Assembly of the United Nations. In the following year a temporary commission was established to supervise free elections throughout the country, but the Russians refused to cooperate and would not even allow the U.N.'s representatives to cross the parallel. In September, 1948, the Soviet Union gave formal recognition to North Korea as the Democratic People's Republic of Korea, with her capital at Pyongyang; and in December the United Nations, realizing the hopelessness of pursuing the matter *de jure,* permitted the creation of the Republic of Korea over the country south of the parallel, but, as yet, without a seat in the United Nations.

Meanwhile, considerable activity was taking place in South Korea where communist guerrillas had infiltrated in large numbers and had tried to cause civil disorder by sabotage, terrorism, and propaganda. But the geographical nature of the country dictated the strategy, and when all else failed the communists risked overt war in order to unite the Korean peninsula under their control. Patrols would have told them of the paucity of the defense. But, by now, China had also become a communist state and, much emboldened, the Sino-Soviet axis evidently felt strong enough to gain by open warfare what it had failed to achieve by subversion. Thus, at dawn on June 25, 1950, North Korea's tanks rumbled southward over the parallel towards Seoul and Wonju.

As a result of the establishment of the two states in Korea, a large number of American troops were withdrawn from the south, leaving only a small advisory force of men whose task was to train the Republic of Korea's Army for the unlikely event of war. But recruitment, training, and reinforcement never matched those of North Korea whose commanders were clearly aware of the designs the Soviet Union had for them.

The element of surprise during the early hours of that Sunday morning was enormous, and the ill-prepared Republic of Korea's Army fell back all along the 150-mile front of the 38th parallel. The communists opened with an intensive and well-coordinated artillery and mortar barrage which hardly gave the South Koreans time to collect their wits and oppose ten infantry divisions, an armored brigade, and other independent units, supported by armament that included 150 T-34 tanks, those stalwarts of World War II and victors over the German Tiger tanks at Kursk in the biggest armored battle ever recorded. The unsuspecting defenders had only four active divisions in reserve positions and could not match the communists' armor.

Later that day the United Nations met in emergency session and passed a resolution, noting "with grave concern the armed attack upon the Republic of Korea by forces from North Korea." The immediate cessation of hostilities and the withdrawal to their original positions beyond the parallel were urged vainly upon the aggressors. Yet, in one respect, the U.N. was fortunate because from the previous January the Soviet delegation had boycotted the Security Council in protest against the Council's refusal to allow Mao Tse-tung's regime to be represented instead of Chiang Kai-shek's Nationalists, so that the remaining members were able to proceed without the hindrance of the Soviet veto. Looking back, it seems extraordinary that Jacob Malik, the Soviet delegate, had not been ordered temporarily to return and effect this diplomatic blockade to assist his allies in Korea to buy time, for Russia had no cause to imagine that the West did not already realize the extent to which it was implicated in the whole affair. But it would only have been a temporary expedient (albeit time enough for the NKPA) because, by Article 51 of the United Nations' Charter, the veto could not prevent a majority of the Security Council from taking action to avoid a critical situation.

Two days later President Truman, in accordance with the United Nations' request that the United States should repel the attack and lead other detachments in defense, ordered moderate air and naval support of the demoralized R.O.K. forces, but this proved to be ineffective. In due course the President ordered the blockade of the entire Korean coast—not the same thing at all as blockading the Chinese coast, which was one of MacArthur's more extravagant ideas. Already, on the day following the outbreak of the offensive, the U.N. Commission on Korea concluded a message to the Secretary-General, Dr. Trygve Lie: ". . . judging from the actual progress of operations the Northern regime is carrying out well planned, concerted and full-scale invason of South Korea; second, that the South Korean forces were deployed on a wholly defensive basis in all sectors of the parallel; and third, that they were taken completely by surprise as they had no reason to believe from intelligence sources that invasion was imminent." [6] MacArthur, who had flown to the front near Seoul (the capture of which he witnessed five days later), had reported to Truman that the South Koreans were hopelessly at odds in morale and performance.

On July 7th, another U.N. resolution explicitly authorized combined military support under the leadership of the United States, the command of which automatically fell to MacArthur. The first American troops who arrived in the peninsula on July 8th (reinforcing the skeleton corps already there, known as *Smithforce*), were the ill-trained and inexperienced 24th Division from Japan, under the command of Maj. Gen. William F. Dean. Meanwhile, the communists' running fight with Lt. Col. C. B. Smith's brave little detachment and the 24th Division, which could not be relied upon to provide seasoned junior officers or N.C.O.'s, provided time for the landing of the 25th Division. The 24th was badly mauled and its commander became the enemy's most senior prisoner throughout the war. But the end of July saw the first integrated resistance to the invaders.

The first weeks of the war had witnessed a military spectacle reminiscent of the overwhelming Japanese victories of late 1941 and early 1942, and they culminated in the gallant defense of the Pusan perimeter, bounded to the west by the Naktong and to the north by a line running from that river to a point on the east coast just north of Pohang-dong. Sufficient Americans had now joined the swiftly conscripted South Koreans to enable the Army commander in Japan and his staff to re-establish themselves on the Korean peninsula still as the Eighth Army. The commander was Gen. Walton H. Walker under whom the withdrawal would go no further. Soldiering under MacArthur's shadow, he has become a sadly neglected figure whose reputation would not be enhanced militarily by the manner and timing of his death. But the Eighth Army obeyed his order to retreat no farther. The fall of the entire Korean peninsula to the Soviet Union and its North Korean satellite would have given immediate prestige to the enemy and placed other non-communist territories—notably Hong Kong, Formosa, Quemoy, and Matsu (which for years afterwards kept up an artillery barrage with the mainland)—in dire peril.

It was during the height of the battle for the perimeter that other U.N. forces began to arrive in Korea. The British advance party included the commander of the 27th Brigade, Brig. B. A. Coad, DSO, who was flown out to Korea while the main body of the Brigade left by sea in the aircraft carrier, HMS *Unicorn*, and the cruiser, HMS *Ceylon*, on August 24th. Altogether, these consisted of: Headquarters 27 Inf. Bde. and Bde. Sig. Tp. (Brig. B. A. Coad, DSO), 1st Bn. The Middlesex Regt. (Lt. Col. A. M. Man, OBE), 1st Bn. Argyll & Sutherland Highlanders (Lt. Col. G. L. Neilson, DSO). Before the winter Canada sent the advance guard of its reinforced infantry brigade which with Australia's two infantry battalions and Britain's two brigades eventually formed the Commonwealth Division.

On September 28th, the British 27th Brigade was joined by the 3rd Bn. Royal Australian Regt. (Lt. Col. C. H. Green, DSO) and on October 1st, it was renamed "The 27th British Commonwealth Infantry Brigade." But this takes us well beyond the initial stages and particularly *Operation Chromite* which was virtually the preserve of the U.S. Marine Corps, except that one has a better idea of MacArthur's international responsibility.

The British Prime Minister, Clement Attlee, had no doubts about the constitutional right of the United Nations, or any of its constituent members, to defend South Korea. The Soviet

Union, however, claimed that in the absence of its own and Chinese communist delegations from the 77-man Security Council the U.N. had no right to act in what was, after all, purely a domestic affair. American intervention was also regarded as illegal because it was *ex post facto* authorization. The Russian Deputy Foreign Minister, Andrei Gromyko, cited the British attack on the Bolsheviks in 1919. "It is universally known how this interventionist adventure ended." [7] And so when the North Koreans, obediently echoing their monolithic neighbor Russia, claimed that they intended to rid their unfortunate comrades of Syngman Rhee's alleged rotten influence, Attlee remarked in typically laconic style, "I am not concerned to defend the [South Korean] Government, or to estimate whether it is good or bad government, but I never knew that an excuse for assaulting someone peacefully pursuing his way was that his character was not very good." [8] Ever consistent with his beliefs, Attlee had invoked the same reason for coming to the defense of Azaña's Republican Government in Spain in 1936. As a statesman he was ever the pragmatist rather than the starry-eyed visionary. After all, Syngman had been properly elected under the auspices of the United Nations, and whatever the nature of his politics that was good enough for Attlee. The Prime Minister shrewdly articulated the allied case in a speech to the House of Commons on July 12th:

> The ordinary principles of international law recognize that any state which is attacked has a right to defend itself, and that any other state has a right to assist the state which is the subject of aggression. The Charter of the United Nations has not taken away this inherent right. On the contrary, it expressly states in Article 51 that "nothing in the present Charter shall impair the inherent right of individual or collective self-defense if an armed attack occurs against a member of the United Nations, until the Security Council has taken the measures necessary to maintain international peace or security." It is true that Article 51 is not to create a new right but merely to make it clear that an inherent right vested in every state is not prejudiced. . . . The broad principle is that all states may be endangered if the aggressor is allowed to get away with the fruits of aggression in any part of the world.[9]

Apart from the United States and South Korea, the United Nations provided 44,000 men, strong because it demonstrated that collective security, as Attlee had signified, was an inherently acceptable principle. The ultimate American Army of 750,000 was the greatest U.S. Army ever committed to war under a single command. These were the ultimate figures on which disappointments at the truce talks had forced greater contribution. For the United States there was also the problem of weighing Europe against Asia. At the outset of the war there was an important section of American opinion—largely Democrats from the New England states—who tended to be the strategic Europhiles, seekers of U.S. protection against the Soviet Union and its Slavic satellites rather than the northern half of an obscure oriental peninsula and its neighbor, Manchuria. Not until two divisions were on the point of being swept into the sea did the United States suddenly wake up and realize that that curious old fellow, MacArthur, was still out there. As his nation's oldest soldier he pleaded for help and it was delivered to him. In the next chapter I will show exactly how hard a task this was to be, even for him. Apart from the U.S. and South Korea, 15 nations eventually made military contributions to the U.N. forces. All fought magnificently together (it must surely have been the only occasion in which Greeks and Turks were allied in war), and the courage of the Turkish Brigade, particularly, will ever be remembered.

By July 27th (three years to the day before the peace was signed at Panmunjom), the threat to Pusan was contained, owing largely to U.S. naval and air support. The cruiser, HMS *Belfast,* flew the flag of the C.-in-C. East Asia Command in the early days of the Korean War and the British naval force, both around the peninsular coast and at Inchon particularly, provided an invaluable contribution. At *Operation Chromite* itself Britain was represented essentially by HMS *Jamaica* and *Kenya,* the former flying the flag of Rear Adm. W. G. Andrewes, RN, commanding the Blockade and Covering Force.

The United States had flown about 10,000 sorties by early August and had thus prevented the communists from coordinating a final offensive. Meanwhile more reserves had arrived, and by September 10th, the enemy's advance was finally halted.

But during the next few days, when the tables were turned, fighting continued to be very heavy while the NKPA deployed 98,000 men in 13 massive infantry divisions, a depleted armored division, two detached armored brigades, and other miscellaneous units. Inside the perimeter were 180,000 men, a large proportion of whom were merely labor units among the Republic of Korea's 92,000. The combat strength of the Americans, with the small cadre of British, totalled 67,000, and the Eighth Army accommodated all soldiers fighting under the United Nations' flag, with its headquarters at Taegu, a road junction narrowly inside the northwest corner of the perimeter. But what troubled MacArthur was the fact that the United Nations was sustaining a thousand casualties a day.

Then suddenly, while the U.N. (particularly the U.S.) was struggling to prevent the biggest embarrassment since Pearl Harbor, MacArthur launched his master stroke. At dawn on September 15th, he watched the U.S. Marine Corps land on the tiny island of Wolmi-do, opposite Inchon harbor, and later that day saw more forces assault the main port itself, inasmuch as it was possible to see anything through the smoke, haze, and gloom. Within a fortnight the vital Kimpo Airfield was retaken and Seoul was handed back to its legitimate government. Two hundred miles behind the front line Inchon was weakly defended by a garrison that had never expected its enemy to attempt such a lunatic operation.

The tidal variation was about 30 feet, permitting the use of the beaches for only about three hours on each tide. This will be described more fully in the next chapter. The tide and the treacherous channel, blockaded by the island, gave MacArthur only six weeks' preparation and training in which thoroughly to familiarize his men with the curious habits of the influx, instead of the six months which such an operation would normally have demanded. For this reason, he rightly argued, the NKPA would be quite unprepared. Moreover, his Marines, once ashore, would have close access to Seoul itself. MacArthur's critics in the Pentagon, with an eye on frustrated public opinion at home, conceded with some apprehension to his request with its confident prediction. As we all know, the operation was a complete success and for this good luck, as always, was partly responsible. The Marines and the Army poured through the gap blown in the enemy's rear, through the capital, and up to the parallel. All this will be related in detail.

The essential redeployment of the NKPA's resources and its fear of the encirclement of its southern armies enabled the Eighth Army to break out of the Pusan perimeter, the failure of which would have presented the Commander in Chief with an embarrassingly difficult problem. But, as it was, the hammer of the Eighth Army smashed on the anvil of X Corps and 125,000 NKPA prisoners were taken. This was a reversal along the lines of the German Spring Offensive in 1918, El Alamein, or Stalingrad. Even war is sweetened by fortune.

Inchon was a daring and brave conception, brilliantly executed and worthy of study as a precedent of amphibious excellence, in the very unlikely case of its ever being considered again as military strategy. David Rees, in his book *Korea: The Limited War,* called it "a twentieth century Cannae, ever to be studied." [10] He was right in the sense that it should never be forgotten. But as immediate events turned out, its benefits were to be completely nullified by Chinese intervention. Cannae, as I have implied, ushered in the Roman conquest of the Mediterranean—albeit about 14 years later—whereas the reversal of the Seoul-Inchon offensive occurred merely two-and-a-half months later; but in principle there was an uncanny similarity so that now, 29 years later, one might treat Inchon as it deserves to be and place it with Salamis, Blenheim, and Waterloo as a battle worthy of minute study for the military mind.

There now followed the most crucial stage of the war, MacArthur's decision, not wholly supported by the Pentagon, to drive on to the Yalu River which forms the southern boundary of Manchuria. At the very least, MacArthur resolved to reach the Chongchon in the west, halting at what became known as "Mig Alley," where the enemy's Mig 15's were later to launch the North Korean aerial defense, and touching the Yalu at two points—at Chosan in the west center and, more thoroughly, at Huesanjin in the east center, which was reached on November 21st by men of the 17th Regiment, U.S. 7th Division. But first MacArthur halted briefly at the 38th parallel to stabilize his position.

The reader will notice from a glance at the map that the length of Korea is divided inland from the east coast by the Taebaek Mountains, which were to frustrate communication between the various units of the advancing U.N. forces. The Inchon landing had been executed by X Corps under Maj. Gen. Edward Almond, with the amphibious support led by Rear Adm. James Doyle, and early on October 17th the Corps was withdrawn from Seoul to seize Wonsan from the sea, over on the east coast. Like Inchon, Wonsan was well behind the enemy's lines. But the advanced units of the Eighth Army (1 and 11 Corps, R.O.K.) had moved so rapidly that they precluded the necessity of amphibious assault.* X Corps, however, landed on October 26th and joined the Eighth Army. But, maintaining his strategy of leapfrogging up the east coast, MacArthur had the 7th Division of the Corps put ashore at Iwon on October 29th, in readiness for the drive to the Yalu. This was positively his last raid from the sea. But at this point MacArthur made the fatal decision to divide the command of his units, giving the eastern sector to Almond and the rest to Walker, while he himself would keep control of them collectively. The mountain range, he reckoned, would in any case make a unified command impossible and he felt that coordination could best be directed from Tokyo. He was subsequently criticized for this when the Chinese "volunteers" were once again to reverse the U.N.'s fortunes and exploit the topographical lack of liaison.

Now MacArthur gave a rather freer interpretation of his orders by the Joint Chiefs of Staff than they would have preferred. General of the Army George Marshall, the new Defense Secretary, had already on September 29th exhorted the Commander in Chief "to feel unhampered" in his operations; but when, on October 24th, MacArthur completely ignored the restraint which he had been advised to put upon non-Korean U.N. forces above the narrow "waist" of North Korea, he elicited some disapproval in the White House and the Pentagon.

* The Eighth Army reached Wonsan on October 10th.

All commanders, he ordered, were "to drive forward with all speed and utilization"; but this, the J.C.S. contended, was "not in consonance" with a directive of September 27th when Seoul was finally cleared of resistance. Certainly the orders Mac-Arthur received were far too imprecise, and such an autocrat needed little excuse to take matters into his own hands. But herein lay the difficulty of having a commander of such seniority, for the J.C.S. felt some constraint in issuing orders to a man who had himself been Chief of Staff of the U.S. Army 20 years earlier. The situation bears no comparison. MacArthur had been ordered "to destroy the North Korean forces," and he did not agree that this could be achieved by leaving the final stages entirely to the South Korean (R.O.K.) Army. He thus invoked Marshall's permission "to feel unhampered." And was Marshall not second only to the President himself in all military matters?

Jubilantly, the Eighth Army swept through Pyongyang, the only iron curtain capital ever occupied by troops of non-communist states, and MacArthur, arriving at the airport on October 20th, inquired facetiously, "Any celebrities here to greet me? Where's Kim Buck Too?" Everyone was optimistic. Mac-Arthur and Walker promised the men that they would be "home by Christmas" (shades of other wars), which was sadly ironic in view of the fact that the latter was to be killed in a jeep accident on the day before Christmas Eve while trying to organize a mammoth retreat which, here and there, had become a rout. But elsewhere the retreat was heroically conducted. Back in the autumn and early winter Brig. Coad had also expressed his belief that the U.N. forces had "cracked the nut" [11] and that it was all over.

But it seems now that MacArthur's great feat was at the same time self-defeating, since a few Chinese units had evidently advanced into North Korea as soon as the Inchon landings had become known in Peking. So Scipio was poised for his thrust at Zama. But the question arises whether the Chinese would have intervened if the United Nations had left a safe buffer zone between their front and the Manchurian border. The Chinese claimed, in that event, that they would not have mobilized their "volunteers"; but one wonders how they could have known of the U.N.'s intentions until the U.N. troops were under orders to advance across the parallel. As mentioned, the U.S. forces reached the Yalu at two points, while the British 27th Brigade reached Chongju, about 40 miles beyond the mouth of the Chongchon on the offending west coast line which the enemy was still vigilantly examining. On the British seaward flank was a brigade of the R.O.K. and on the eastern side a division composed of Americans and Turks.

The United Nations had barely gained its farthest limit when the Chinese, who had already struck at various isolated points, swept down in force upon the right flank of the Eighth Army where, along the western foothills of the Taebaek Range, liaison with X Corps was weak. Walker temporarily withheld the onslaught on the left, but part of the 180,000-strong horde smashed unskillfully through three of the right flank R.O.K. divisions and threatened to invest the army, thus obliging the U.N. to retreat from the whole length of the Chongchon River. The "volunteers," even such a ragged bunch as this, must have been poised below the Yalu before September 15th, and it was one of MacArthur's complaints that he was not allowed to keep a vigil from the skies over Manchuria during this period.

Since this sudden reversal occurred about a month before Christmas it was evident that all hope of reaching the Yalu along the entire front and packing up in time for Christmas was no longer possible, and all effort was devoted to withdrawing the Eighth Army to fresh lines. The retreat, particularly from the Chosin Reservoir, was under the circumstances a remarkably well conducted operation which witnessed many acts of gallantry. The privations which the men endured, comparable with the agonizing retreat from Moscow of the armies of Napoleon and Hitler, were aggravated by the onset of a North Korean winter when temperatures have been known to fall nearly to −40° where the centigrade and fahrenheit scales join forces in a concerted assault upon body and soul. The burial of the dead, in the hasty retreat, was achieved only with bulldozers in the permafrost which lay just beneath the surface of rock-hard earth. So incised, it swallowed up in mass anonymous graves Americans, British, Canadians, Australians, Turks, countless South Koreans, and others—now a truly integrated force of united nations. Morale among the U.N. forces was desperately low, and in so remote a part of the world it was obviously difficult to make the men, particularly the non-Koreans, believe in so apparently nebulous a cause as that which the unified command represented.

The Chinese had to rely on sheer weight of numbers, and hastily recruited as the bulk of their army was, its training was minimal and fieldcraft non-existent, except inasmuch as they tried to create fear in a most unorthodox way which, left unchecked in some victims, had almost a psychotic effect. The enemy usually made no attempt at concealment, which in any case was difficult in a landscape which gave as much cover as that afforded to an ant on a white blanket. For much of the night the communists would make their sinister presence felt by playing amplified records, for example, of Al Jolson singing *Mammy* (Jolson himself died from pneumonia contracted while visiting the American forces in Korea in 1950) for the sake of nostalgia. Towards the end of the war the repertoire had been extended to include the voice of America's favorite young pin-up, a certain Marilyn Monroe who sang the capitalist's creed about diamonds being a girl's best friend. For the British brigades, persuasion was pre-war; a smart rendering of *Colonel Bogey* or *If You Were the Only Girl in the World* were intended to crack morale. The whole spectacle was both sinister and ludicrous. In the dawn light of the North Korean winter the Chinese would appear, massed and dun, against the snow-clad hills which rose in countless undulations like the waves of a heavy sea. Then the enemy would signal their assault by blowing whistles and banging gongs, frequently advancing right under their own artillery "stonks," which were hardly surprising tactics for a people who place so little value on individual life. Occasionally the frozen corpses of women, still clutching Russian-made rifles, were found among the carnage left behind. Today such a sight would hardly cause the surprise this caused the U.N. troops. The communists' service corps was a pathetic shambles, for they seemed to have virtually no motorized transport. Heavy machine guns and ammunition boxes were frequently rushed up by waves of elderly men, women, and children, bowed under the weight. They were reminiscent of the Republicans in the Spanish Civil War. If the Chinese and North Koreans were unable to achieve their objectives, they could not easily extricate themselves, so that immediate counterattacks usually bagged more prisoners than could conveniently be collected; although it was often difficult to see who was who. Occasionally dedicated communists would change into the uniforms of dead R.O.K. troops and infiltrate the U.N. positions. Such was the repetitive, if unnerving, pattern of the infantryman's life, until the opposing forces dug in for the static war of the last two years, which in itself has too frequently been underrated and overlooked.

To all veterans of the Korean War the smell of human excrement, with which the Koreans fertilized their fields, will transport the vanished warrior at once to that bare hilly country, animated only by lone farmers in flat conical hats with yokes of water buffalo and expressionless faces, revealing a strange indifference to fate. The European soldier will remember the destitute land which, to the memory's eye, seemed always to be subject to various stages of night-time when stealthy silent patrols were moving as in a statuesque trance.

The communists kept allied prisoners in the most inhuman conditions in several camps across North Korea, of which that known as *The Caves* was probably the most notorious. The United Nations, by contrast, herded the enemy's P.O.W.s into 6 camps on Koje Island off the south coast where there was never a hint of maltreatment. But a sixth column organized concerted riots there in February, 1952, and in the ensuing riots enemy prisoners sustained 85 fatal and 116 wounded casualties among their demonstrators from which the Chinese and NKPA made as much capital as they could. Unfortunately they captured the camp commandant, Brig. Gen. Dodd, as a hostage. This was the climax of the Koje-do insurrection, occurring on May 7th, shortly before Ridgway was due to hand over command to Gen. Mark Clark.* Despite harsh terms

* It is interesting to see how fortune altered the seniority of these two officers. In World War II, General Mark Clark had commanded the 5th Army in Italy and was Deputy Supreme Commander in that theater to Field Marshal Alexander. Ridgway, however, commanded only a division

Dodd's life was spared and he was relieved of his responsibility. Order was regained and the outgoing commander was able to hand over an orderly command to his successor, but not before the much tried Admiral C. Turner Joy had asked to be relieved of his task at Panmunjom and had been succeeded, on May 22, 1952, by Lt. Gen. William K. Harrison who drew up the eventual armistice.

In the spring of 1952 the emphasis of the U.N.'s strategy was switched to selected aerial bombardment. Sabrejets and Shooting Stars dropped napalm extensively for the first time and American pilots became the least fortunate prisoners of war, being tortured remorselessly to confess to the use of non-existent bacteriological weapons. But for most prisoners, of course, the kid glove was used to turn captives into communists. For the first time we heard of the expression "brainwashing," * whereby the prisoners' minds were intended to be emptied of every preconception and fundamental belief so that they could be filled instead with communist and Marxist ideology.[12]

But to return to the specific situation at the end of 1950 which had silenced the euphoria of the Inchon-Seoul operation, MacArthur complained bitterly, and perhaps justifiably, that he had been forbidden to use aerial reconnaissance over Manchuria in order to assess Chinese reaction to the U.N.'s advance; but then he had earlier claimed that no right-thinking Chinese general would attempt to cross the Yalu in winter. In this connection one should cite the evidence (at the MacArthur hearings which occurred after the General's recall), of the Air

---

and then a corps in France and Holland, but being responsible to the JCS for following the Korean strategy, he was the automatic choice to succeed Walker and then MacArthur. Thereafter, nothing less than command of SHAPE was adequate, while Clark was still fulfilling Ridgway's old duties in Korea and the Far East. Finally Ridgway became the Army's Chief of Staff, a post which eluded Clark, a veteran of France and Flanders in General Pershing's expeditionary force.

* The term was first used by the American journalist Edward Hunter in *Brainwashing in Red China* (1951). It is a translation of the Chinese colloquialism *hsi nao* (wash brain). It should be avoided because the various processes known loosely by the term are called in official Chinese communist dogma *szu-hsiang kai-tsao*, meaning "ideological" or "thought" reform.

Force Chief, Gen. Hoyt Vandenberg, who had been a sharp critic of MacArthur's over-ambitious offensive from Seoul to the Chongchon. Vandenberg reckoned that the U.S.A.F. could attack either China or Russia, but not both; and he feared that MacArthur's reconnaissances would soon become offensive sorties which, he felt, would not be sufficiently conclusive. Vandenberg dared not risk his "shoe string" Air Force, which he saw as the United States' greatest deterrent to war. To bomb China, he claimed, would simply be "to peck at the periphery" [13] of an enormous target with few worthwhile military installations. In the absence of reconnaissance, MacArthur complained, he could use only his land forces to determine the existence, strength, and disposition of the Chinese. But in that case he must be blamed for adopting such a sanguine attitude and for failing to be prepared militarily to meet the unspoken threat of invasion from China, blame which Walker must share. On December 23rd, as mentioned, Walker himself was killed in a jeep accident, and with his Eighth Army trying desperately to hold the line of the 38th parallel he was replaced by Lt. Gen. Matthew B. Ridgway, the distinguished parachute commander of World War II. The luckless defender of Pusan was posthumously made a four-star general. On New Year's Eve the communists began their second invasion of South Korea.

By now the Chinese strength had increased to 400,000, which was assisted by a new army of 100,000 North Koreans. The United Nations, infinitely better equipped, had 200,000 men, about half of whom were American. They continued to fall back south and southeast of Seoul, but by the nature of their tactics the communists suffered astronomic losses. Slowly Ridgway stiffened the resistance south of Seoul, but the enemy drove a wedge down the center towards Wonju. By mid-January, with the help of superior air cover, the United Nations had stabilized the line and wasted no time in launching a counterattack which Ridgway, in keeping with the J.C.S. preference, directed against selected areas. It was very evident that after the disaster on the Chongchon, when he was obliged to obey the President and the J.C.S. more readily, MacArthur willingly delegated authority to his new subordinate and remained rather pathetically aloof, attending to his other business in Tokyo. During his last four months abroad he made little personal impact upon the Korean War, although he visited the front both to raise morale in retreat and share the jubilation of advance. But what one might call the Heroic Stage of the war was clearly over.

Carefully the Eighth Army probed forward, and a month later had taken the vital "Iron Triangle" formed by the towns of Chorwon, Kumhwa and Pyonggang (*not* Pyongyang) which was the major communist assembly and supply area. Although by the end of May the communists had completed another offensive to which the United Nations had replied, the line was now reaching its last resting place, to be varied only a little here and there, until the final armistice at Panmunjom. It was during the communist offensive towards the end of April, 1951, that Brig. Brodie's 29th Brigade in general and the 1st Bn. The Gloucestershire Regt. in particular so distinguished themselves, the latter near Solma-ri on Hill 235 (Gloster Hill), above the Imjin River, inspiring the new Eighth Army commander, Lt. Gen. James Van Fleet, to describe the action as "the most outstanding example of unit bravery in modern warfare." Uttered by their American commander, the British could find this praise indeed, of which they were utterly worthy.

Van Fleet, the General who was actively concerned with the Korean War for longer than any other, had replaced Ridgway when the latter succeeded MacArthur as the Commander in Chief, Far East, and of the United Nations Command. He was, for most of his command, to lack only MacArthur's proconsular authority because later in 1951, the Japanese peace treaty * removed power over Japan and returned it to Tokyo. Mac-Arthur's dismissal had occurred, not altogether unexpectedly, on April 11, 1951. The General had been in the Far East continuously, without home leave (except for a few weeks' home leave in 1937), for 14 years, since, after his period as Chief of Staff of the U.S. Army, he had been sent by Roosevelt to command the Philippine garrison of the United States Army at Luzon in 1935. He was thus persuaded to believe that the ultimate east-west conflict (regarded as more

* The treaty was signed on September 8, 1951, and ratified on April 28, 1952.

immediate and less victorious then than it is today) would not be in Europe—as Truman, Bradley, and others believed—but in the Far East. The witness of Pearl Harbor would not be caught a second time. His unchallenged authority had become entrenched, and his erstwhile enemies—ever lovers of a victor—had become his strongest admirers; indeed, when Hirohito went to bid MacArthur farewell the Emperor broke down. This curious chivalry toward MacArthur by the Japanese was reciprocated, as Averell Harriman recorded when he found the General evidently disturbed and revealing "strong emotion" at the impending execution of Yamashita, adjudged by the Supreme Allied Court in Tokyo.* There will be further evidence in this book that MacArthur readily succumbed to emotion. As a military proconsul the old General outstripped even Kitchener in his duration of continuous command abroad. His record was remarkable.

The son of Gen. Arthur MacArthur, a former military governor of the Philippines, he had graduated first in his class at West Point with the highest marks ever recorded and had originally served in Korea as early as 1905. Having commanded a division in France in 1917-18, when he was the youngest general in the American Army, he became Chief of the U.S. Sector of the Rhine. Various commands took him eventually to that of Chief of Staff of the U.S. Army by the age of 50 (1930–35),† after which he took the President's discretionary and extraordinary post in the Philippines. The General took home leave for his second marriage in 1937 before returning to the Pacific. That year saw his formal retirement from the Army, but the expansion of Japanese influence was far too great a menace to allow him to retreat passively to the United States, and while little appeared to be done by way of actual progress towards firm defense in the Pacific, MacArthur was able to convince a very run-down command that he had the situation in hand, so far as supply allowed. Korea must have seemed like *déjà vu*. The attack on Pearl Harbor thus found him in Manila, pending the necessity of a swift retreat. But his Pacific record in

---

* Like Churchill, MacArthur tended, quite unashamedly, to be subject to catharsis.

† This appointment goes right back to President Hoover.

World War II, when Field Marshal Alanbrooke regarded him as "the greatest general of the last war," [14] is well known. After accepting the formal Japanese surrender on board the USS *Missouri* in Tokyo Bay on September 2, 1945, aged 65, he remained in Toyko with the newly created rank of General of the Army from which, like that of field marshal, there is no statutory retiring age. Only Marshall and Eisenhower (a major on his staff in 1934) have likewise been promoted. Thus he was well into his 71st year when the Korean War broke out, but his age seemed to have no adverse effects, for physically and mentally he was a model of alertness. And so his authority was not questioned by Truman when the United Nations sought American leadership in Korea. But he was inflexible.

MacArthur resembled Churchill and, as he would have liked to believe, his own hero, James Wolfe, in his eccentric appraisal of military adversity. It is hardly too extravagant to describe as genius his flair for unorthodoxy, like Hannibal's, but founded upon sound training and much experience. His impressive achievements against Japan bore the same Napoleonic stamp which would carry Inchon and Seoul and rout the investors of Pusan. I believe that he was the greatest American general at least since Robert E. Lee, and I am prepared to sacrifice objectivity to make that assessment. But if comparisons are odious it was by an extraordinary paradox that, of all the allied commanders in 1950, only MacArthur, by far the most experienced, would have been so self-confident and decisive as unwittingly to erode the power of command in the field, for there has been no such military autocrat since. Only a man so senior that he had to drop seniority by 20 years in order to become commander in chief could exist at the time to illustrate that in the new atomic age no nation could ever again afford to employ so totally resourceful a commander. But if it should be argued that MacArthur brought the world to the brink of atomic war it could more logically be explained that the General eroded that same atomic danger by conscripting a vast conventional force of Marines and G.I.'s which he would vitally need at Inchon. I refer to this aspect more thoroughly in the next chapter. Success thereafter halted the atomic bias, evident between 1945 and 1950, which, under the stewardship of Louis Johnson, was shredding all the U.S. services but the Air Force and weakening their ability to fight a limited war, paradoxically what MacArthur least envisaged. But MacArthur could not even give the appearance of espousing atomic war. Like Joab, he could not disobey the King's orders, and like King David, Truman had to be seen ultimately to command his army.

MacArthur's advanced years were to reveal themselves in other ways during the early months of the war, since he had naturally been brought up to believe that victory or defeat alone determined the outcome of military conflict. He must have felt the early defeats more keenly than anyone. His tendency to disregard imprecise orders if they seriously conflicted with his own beliefs has already been mentioned. The reversal on the Chongchon was serious enough, but Truman may not have decided to recall the Commander in Chief had he not continued to advocate measures which, to the President, the J.C.S., and the British Government, seemed extremely perilous to world peace. MacArthur appeared to be challenging the very supremacy of the President. In his public statement, as we have seen, Truman announced his decision with tact and diplomacy, no doubt to avoid alienating the Republican waverers as much as to accommodate the convictions of his veteran commander. MacArthur had urged the bombing of Chinese bases in Manchuria,[15] in addition to the reconnaissance of them (about which we have noted Vandenberg's reaction) as the only method of curbing the continued resistance of China. Of course, MacArthur's idea of China's military potential, judged on the basis of his long experience of the East, and Vandenberg's, were inevitably different. But, more dangerously still, he wanted to blockade the Chinese coast and introduce Chinese Nationalists to the U.N. forces. No doubt, the thought of using Japanese troops crossed his mind but he must have dismissed this while the Japanese peace treaty from the Second World War remained unsigned. At Inchon, however, he did use some heavily armed Japanese landing craft, manned by his former enemies, but fortunately no further questions were asked. These will be mentioned in due course.

But from a strictly military point of view MacArthur could

argue with evident logic and a sense of reality. The United States was still undoubtedly the greatest military power in the world, in nuclear and conventional weapons, although the Soviet Union had detonated its first nuclear device, according to President Truman who made the announcement on October 23, 1949. Parity between the powers was more evident when it was confirmed that the Soviet Union's first thermonuclear bomb had been monitored on August 12, 1953, having been declared by Malenkov four days earlier. This was only about a fortnight after the Korean War had ended on a note of atomic threat by Eisenhower. But, however reckless he may have been, MacArthur could still argue from a position of undoubted strength. Communist China, ever the sinister and enigmatic threat, was still believed to be weak after its war with Japan closely followed by internal disruption. This would be the last chance of preventing its ascendency to mammoth proportions. (I take no account of current diplomacy in 1979.)

To the other leaders, however, all this was less evident, and to the Democrat Truman in particular, MacArthur, the traditional Republican, was presenting a direct threat to his authority. The President did not tell his senior colleagues this when on April 6th he sought their advice. This has been mentioned. But while Truman may have wondered why he had not sacked MacArthur years before, he did say in a news conference on May 17th that he had considered replacing MacArthur over a year before his final decision. Had that been so, and with all other records running to form (and there is no evidence that they would not), there would, for good or ill, certainly have been no Inchon. Apparently Truman's mind was finally made up by MacArthur's declared ultimatum of March 24th that the Chinese commander Peng Teh-huai would have to surrender his volunteer force to the United Nations or face all-out aggression by the United States.[16] President Eisenhower was to make the same threat a little over two years later, and if the communist reaction to obey was so swift on that occasion, their more advanced technique notwithstanding, how much more readily would they have responded had the ultimatum been Truman's. But the fact that the ultimatum did not come from the man at the top was an indication that the enemy, at least, knew who was who, even if the President could not trust in the common sense of his own people to know who ultimately conducted the orchestra. Perhaps Truman and MacArthur should have made a greater effort at reconciliation where the threat to the President was less real than he believed. Or perhaps MacArthur was just a brilliant anachronism whose dismissal assured the Republican party of victory in the next White House elections. The lack of trust between Truman and MacArthur tempted the latter unwisely to conduct affairs at his personal discretion. A letter from MacArthur to the opposition leader in the House of Representatives, which was made public on April 5th, supported the use of Chinese Nationalist troops in Korea. Here was a threat far more dangerous than the unlikelihood of atomic warfare, for their use would have invited a communist retaliatory attack on Formosa (as it was then known). Truman discovered the letter and reacted less than a week later.

But public opinion in the United States, tiring in any case of a Democrat as President, which they had experienced since 1932, was less informed and less adamant. When New Yorkers eventually welcomed their hero home (still to be acclaimed for his victories over the Japanese) the volume of ticker tape they deposited, amounting to 3,249 tons, was almost double the previous record held in the name of the pioneer Atlantic aviator, Charles Lindbergh.

But for MacArthur's decisiveness and long, unique reputation it is certain that events in Korea would have been very different and the President and his colleagues would have been able to impose their will more easily. Yet there would have been no Inchon and it is doubtful, with casualties mounting at the rate of a thousand men a day, whether Walker's brave defense of the Pusan perimeter could have been sustained without the diversionary offensive. On the other hand, Chinese "volunteers" would not (so we are to suppose) have become involved. But all this is hypothetical. As it was, Inchon must be regarded as the military and diplomatic turning point of the war. From its brilliant success, yet quite unexpected and disastrous aftermath, there arose the more compliant commands of Ridgway and Mark Clark under whom limited warfare became a strange but practical reality.

An important occasion of the war, not yet mentioned, but which occurred as a direct result of Inchon, was the meeting between Truman and MacArthur on Wake Island in the Pacific on October 15, 1950. Regarded by some as a victory conference and by others as an opportunity for acrimony, it was the only time the two men ever met. It seems remarkable that the President should have travelled three-quarters of the way towards his subordinate's domain rather than have requested MacArthur to visit him in Washington. This must have strengthened still further the General's belief in his own indispensability and superiority in all but rank. One might have understood it if Truman had gone right on to visit the men at the front. Perhaps he felt that his overall unpopularity would be reinforced rather than eroded by such a gesture, for even after the retreat from the Chongchon, MacArthur remained a legendary figure among the ordinary U.S. servicemen. If Truman had so decided the decision would have been political rather than personal, for he was no moral coward; indeed, only 25 years later he was to become a cult figure of the White House, so appreciated had his honesty become. Roosevelt had received MacArthur at Hawaii in 1944, but now the General chose Wake Island as a suitable place to receive his President.

From old film of the occasion it can be seen that MacArthur, however cordial, did not salute his Commander in Chief when Truman stepped from the Presidential aircraft. The Inchon landing had occurred a month earlier and the U.N. forces, having crossed the parallel, were poised for their thrust to the Yalu. The weekend of the meeting was also allegedly that on which the Chinese decided to send their first troops into Korea. Truman had brought a large retinue with him, including Averell Harriman, the President's Assistant, Dean Rusk (the Deputy Secretary of State) and Gen. Bradley. Even as the Chinese were tentatively crossing the frontier (for MacArthur's air reconnaissance over North Korea itself revealed nothing which gave him cause for concern) the two leaders speculated on the problem that was at the back of everyone's mind. The exchange went thus:

TRUMAN: What are the chances for Chinese or Soviet intervention?

MACARTHUR: Very little. Had they interfered in the first or second months it would have been decisive. We no longer stand hat in hand. The Chinese have 300,000 men in Manchuria. Of these probably not more than 100,000-125,000 are distributed along the Yalu River.* They have no air force. Now that we have bases for our air force in Korea, if the Chinese tried to get down to Pyongyang there would be the greatest slaughter. . . .[17]

Clearly, MacArthur did not foresee the speed and strength of the enemy's assault. Of more likely threat was the Russian Air Force with its powerful MIG-15's, but MacArthur dismissed this because he did not believe that a Sino-Soviet alliance was feasible. Here was a fundamental danger in having in command a man with such customary and traditional views on the Orient, founded on personal experience and the collective belief of several generations. It was this break with tradition which caused the old General to write to the U.N. of "an entirely new war." [18] Unknown to MacArthur, a complete transcript had been taken of the meeting, and several of his optimistic contentions were quoted back to him during the hearings that followed his recall. The age of "bugging" had begun, and the unwitting were made pathetic by the ravages of science.

By the middle of 1951 the Democrats were severely assaulted from every side. Truman and the Secretary of State, Dean Acheson, in particular, were regarded as the arch-villains for pursuing an allegedly timid, circuitous, and protracted campaign, rather than going all-out for victory. It seemed almost as if Truman were trying to placate the conscience he had had, perforce, to disturb when he ordered the bombing of Hiroshima and Nagasaki. To him war was not the honorable skill of arms which was the long experience of his veteran commander, and it seemed that the American people did not appreciate their difference of outlook. The mid-term elections

* On November 28, 1950, after four days of full offensive, MacArthur informed the U.N. that "Chinese continental forces . . . of an aggregate strength of 200,000 men are now arrayed against the United Nations' forces in North Korea. . . ." (From the MacArthur Hearings, p. 1834.)

were a severe setback for the ruling Democrats in the Senate, where their majority fell from 92 to 36. Among the new Republican senators was Richard Nixon of California, triumphant after his successful prosecution of the spy, Alger Hiss, and one who particularly castigated the new compliant policy in Korea. This was also the genesis of the McCarthy "witch hunts" for followers of "un-American activities." In the months ahead the Democrats were to suffer increasing criticism, and there is no doubt that Eisenhower's election to the presidency in 1952 was determined chiefly by the Korean issue, made pertinent by his own military distinction.

From December 5–7, 1952, the President-elect implemented a promise to visit Korea, which Truman had never done. Eisenhower told the troops that the cessation of hostilities would be his prior aim, but cessation with honor. That went down very well. But when, by the spring of 1953, the deadlock over the prisoner of war issue had still not been broken at the Panmunjom truce talks, Eisenhower let it be known to Peking via Indian diplomatic channels that unless the United Nations' reasonable and last negotiated offer (the talks, initiated at Kaesong, had been in progress since July 8, 1951) was accepted, the United States would consider extending the war, by which he euphemistically meant the use of nuclear weapons. Only this fear, it seems, moved the communists to end hostilities. I have already referred to the issue. It was a terrible risk which, in real terms, far exceeded anything which Truman would have sanctioned, and one that could never be repeated. Perhaps it joins the Soviet Union's attempt to send atomic warheads to Cuba as the two most dangerous and precipitate situations since World War II.

But what was the essence of the policy which Truman preferred to pursue against the inevitability of losing office? The President was a courageous man; his dismissal of MacArthur testified to that. And now he knew that he was gambling his career on an unpopular strategy, and losing. As a result of the Chinese intervention and the traumatic offensives which followed, Truman was determined to limit the war and give the least chance for the communists to accuse the Americans of undue aggression. From that moment the prospect of total war receded, and no subsequent threat to world peace, whatever the accompanying tumult, has been as sinister as in the early days of the Korean War when the chief combatants faced each other in naked aggression and unguarded hostility. I have already mentioned the extent to which American airmen were tortured to make specious confessions of guilt. It was supposed that they were implementing horrific U.N. plans to eliminate North Korean forces. That this should have occurred at all is an unfortunate indication of the success of Truman's peaceful overtures when the enemy was not interested in peace. Frustrating though limited war was to the military leaders, Truman had the support—or at least the understanding—of his Joint Chiefs of Staff and most of the senior commanders in Korea. The President was determined to return to the *status quo ante bellum*, and even the communists, for less altruistic reasons, had realized the hopelessness of conquering South Korea at least on that occasion. Whether or not the United Nations could have won with an all-out offensive, which would have included the bombing of Manchurian depots and supply routes, without at the same time risking a third world war, the American leaders decided that they would not risk it, but instead would wage an interminable war of attrition and containment, while the talks proceeded along a front which was reminiscent of France and Flanders.

Truman doubtless knew the treatises of von Clausewitz, a vital extract from whose work *Vom Kriege* applies here:

> That the political point of view should end completely when war begins would only be conceivable if wars were struggles of life or death, from pure hatred. As wars are in reality, they are . . . only the manifestations of policy itself. The subordination of the political point of view to the military would be unreasonable, for policy is the intelligent faculty, war only the instrument, and not the reverse. The subordination of the military point of view to the political is, therefore, the only thing which is possible.[19]

That, it seems, would exactly concur with Truman's own belief. For him the threat of the atomic bomb was the only reasonable alternative, because it assured a ready return to the intelligent faculty which existed somewhere in the *status quo ante bellum*.

While MacArthur confessedly abhorred war, his own reluctant strategy was more aggressive than Truman's. If war were inevitable, then every political consideration should be put aside and all energy devoted to ending the military conflict as soon as possible. War and peace were two utterly different species rather than a severe cleavage under pressure of some common force. MacArthur's ultimate and unconfirmed strategic intentions apart, the object of halting aggression had been the whole impulse behind Inchon. It was these thoughts which MacArthur expressed in a memorable speech to Congress on April 19, 1951, immediately after his return. The address was eloquent and moving; ranging, sometimes optimistically, over many Far Eastern problems, for he had not had the opportunity to address such an audience since the end of World War II. He would not be swayed by what he called the "Die for Tie" strategy. But the nub of his beliefs about Korea was contained in the following extract:

> It has been said in effect that I was a warmonger. Nothing could be further from the truth. I know war as few other men now living know it, and nothing, to me, is more revolting. I have long advocated its complete abolition,* as its very destructiveness on both friend and foe has rendered it useless as a means of settling international disputes. . . .† But once war is forced upon us, there is no alternative than to apply every available means to bring it to a swift end. . . . War's very object is victory. There are some, who, for varying reasons, would appease Red China. They are blind to history's clear lesson, for that lesson teaches, with unmistakable emphasis, that appeasement only begets new and bloodier wars. It points to no single instance where this end has justified that means, where appeasement has led to more than a sham peace. Like blackmail, violence becomes the only alternative. Why, my soldiers asked me, surrender military advantage to an enemy in the field? I could not answer. . . .

* There is a certain naiveté and facility in the expression of this belief, no matter how sincerely meant.

† MacArthur may have thought otherwise when he went to bed on September 15, 1950.

Yet today the vast proliferation of wars proves their limited application. The Inchon-Seoul offensive was, I repeat, the last great amphibious operation and planned pitched battle the world will probably ever experience. War has changed. Seen in the context of old wars Korea was neither lost nor won. President Eisenhower expressed the position in a broadcast to his people following the ceasefire: "We have won an armistice on a battleground, not peace in the world. We may not now relax our guard nor cease our quest." [20] Of course, he was right; as subsequent history in Korea alone has amply borne out.

The campaigns of 1952 and 1953, too often overlooked in histories of the Korean War, were those of the limited war in its infancy when the front hovered around the 38th parallel and the two sides conferred first at Kaesong from July 10, 1951, and after a temporary breakdown, at Panmunjom from October 25, 1951, until an armistice was signed on July 27, 1953. Nevertheless, constant patrolling and some harsh fighting took place, and veterans will particularly remember Luke the Gook's Castle, Heartbreak Ridge, Jane Russell Hill, Old Baldy, and a curiously shaped cluster of hills called the Hook, a British preserve and the very last set-piece battle in military history which was held against mammoth communist assaults in the early winter of 1952 and the late spring of the following year. The last contended piece of Korea was at the American salient around Pork Chop Hill in May, 1953, when, at the last minute, the communists succeeded in regaining an area of real estate, as it could absurdly be called, which an intrusive U.S. patrol seemed likely to nip off. The NKPA and their Chinese allies hoped to rape as much country as possible in the face of the now pending and inevitable peace.

And today, while wars become more insidious, we are strangely aware of the lack of formal military hostilities among the more powerful states in relation to the deep factions which undoubtedly exist as powerfully as ever. Since 1945 we have had to suffer what should be called the Second World Peace. Meanwhile we should pause to consider whether this farewell to arms is real or delusive. Professor Michael Howard, in his book *Studies in War and Peace*, asserts that "Politicians must now interpenetrate military activity as thoroughly as the nervous system penetrates the tissues of the human body. . . . ," and predicts that "Regiments will bear as their battle honours, not the battles they have fought, but those they have averted." He speaks with the same happy hypothesis as Gen. MacArthur abolishing war. Are we entering a new Elysian age which may trace its impulse from the battlefields of Korea, or has the prospect of atomic war made us talk in self-fooling riddles? Is all this, perhaps, just another (albeit very eloquent) way of saying, "Peace at any price"?

But for the vortex of modern military thinking, or the fulcrum on which the future was balanced, we must return to the early months of the Korean War when soldiers were still sanguine and U.S. morale (not so easily subvertible as it was shown to be in Vietnam) responded to sound leadership and kept in good order even during the terrible retreat from the Chongchon. We must return to the twilight of the military commander as a decisive force, and so to the last great amphibious battle in history—Inchon.

CHAPTER TWO

The "5,000-to-1 Gamble"*

We now know something of the attitude of Gen. MacArthur toward his enemies in Korea and to his colleagues in the Pentagon. We have long known of his autocracy and self-confidence which, of all his great military contemporaries, could perhaps be matched only by that of Montgomery of Alamein, although the British field marshal would not have adopted such an apparently reckless plan as the Inchon landing. It was MacArthur himself who, in a facetious phrase which he later regretted, described the landings as having "a 5,000-to-1" chance of success, although he was to sway the experienced diplomat, Averell Harriman, Gen. Lawrence Norstad (later Allied Commander, Europe) and Lt. Gen. Matthew B. Ridgway with his rhetoric, clear reasoning, and astonishing military insight. This chapter, therefore, will be devoted chiefly to arguments for and against the Inchon landing and of how MacArthur managed to disabuse his critics—the President and the Joint Chiefs of Staff—and so be allowed to execute the venture with his trusted subordinate, Maj. Gen. Edward M. Almond.† This persuasion was about MacArthur's most difficult task; and certainly it deserves a chapter of its own before we land with the 3/5th Marines on

---

* "I realize that Inchon is a 5000-to-1 gamble, but I am used to taking such odds. . . ." (Gen. MacArthur)

† Attention will be drawn to a criticism of MacArthur's appointing Almond to this dual role, especially since Almond was an Army general whose chief responsibility lay over a Marine division. Almond's deputy, as opposed to Chief of Staff, was Maj. Gen. Clark Ruffner.

the island of Wolmi-do (designated Green Beach), for no comparable offensive in modern history has had to be placed with greater precision.

According to Ridgway, *Operation Chromite* was a typical MacArthur expedition from inception to execution. "While others thought of a way to withdraw our forces safely MacArthur planned for victory." [1] And another commentator of the war, the verbose staff officer Maj. Gen. Charles Willoughby,* U.S. Army, wrote: "MacArthur courageously set his sights on a greater goal; to salvage the reputation of allied arms, to bring into sharper focus the colossal threat of imperialist mongoloid pan-Slavism under the guise of Communism, and to smash its current challenge in one great blow." [2]

The Commander in Chief had first conceived the idea of assaulting Inchon from the sea as early as June 29th when, from an aerial view† on the same melancholy occasion as when he had watched the capture of Seoul, he foresaw the over-attenuating lines of supply which the communists were creating for themselves. As the line lengthened, he would hit the enemy where they least expected it, and where better than at the nearest seaport to the capital, Seoul, which was only 18 miles due eastward? He recalled how he had outflanked an entire Japanese Army in this way by leapfrogging 500 miles along the northern New Guinea coast in 1942.

This was the broad strategy which he was determined to follow. The predecessor to *Operation Chromite* was *Operation Bluehearts*, but the essential difference was that in the latter and more ambitious case, which MacArthur duly scrapped, the idea was to put the 1st Cavalry Division ashore as early as July 20th; but this was precluded ten days earlier by the rapid advance of the NKPA, so that the division had to be sent instead to Pohang-dong. This was also the day when Lt. Gen.

---

* Né Tscheppe-Weidenbach, who had been MacArthur's Intelligence Officer since 1941, still spoke with a strong German accent. He and Whitney competed for authority about MacArthur, but Whitney's biography is generally preferred.

† The General was in no danger because the U.S. was in complete command of the sky.

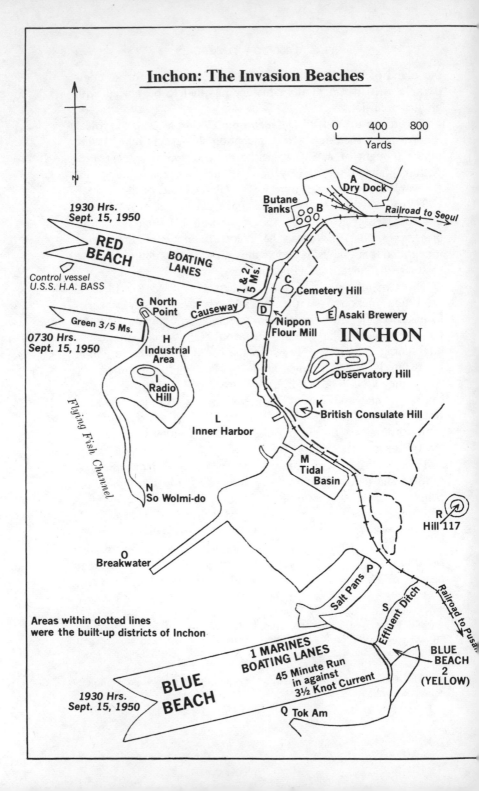

Inchon: The Invasion Beaches

Lemuel C. Shepherd, the new Marine Fleet Commander in the Pacific, told MacArthur in Tokyo that, subject to J.C.S. approval, it would be possible to get the entire 1st Marine Division to Korea in six weeks and in action by September 15th. Mention will be made in the course of this chapter to Marine logistics to comply with *Chromite*.

Among all the planning and strategic theorizing, one important matter had yet to be considered. Public opinion at home was an unknown quantity. While the President could authorize the draft of young and as yet untrained men who might only be of marginal value against the evident power of North Korea, he was for political reasons very reluctant to call back veterans of World War II who probably felt that they had done their bit and were at last settling into new civilian jobs. Only the long lines of volunteers for re-enlistment with the Marines at Camp Pendleton testified to the devotion of these veterans to the Marine Corps, their realization of the importance of the task for which they were needed and the almost deified regard in which they held General MacArthur, either by repute or personal experience of his leadership.

He never doubted his own judgment (except, as we will see, when he wondered whether he should have chosen Kunsan), but there remained two particularly daunting tasks, persuading the service chiefs to accept his scheme and obtaining sufficient men to be deployed in the right place at the right time and all with adequate training to the occasion. Maj. Gen. O. P. Smith, commander of the 1st Marine Division, left the United States on August 18th, and was fortunate in having a pre-conference and informal discussion with MacArthur, for he had reached Tokyo four days later. Next day MacArthur seriously got to grips with at least one of his tasks when he held what was the essential conference on *Chromite* at 1730 hours on August 23rd in his office on the sixth floor of the Dai Ichi Building, his headquarters in Tokyo. If ever he possessed powers of advocacy, reason, optimism, and boundless courage, this is where and when he would need them.

Those who attended the conference on April 23rd were the commanders in chief, Far East Naval and Air Forces, Vice-Adm. C. Turner Joy and Lt. Gen. George E. Stratemeyer;

MacArthur's Chief of Staff, Maj. Gen. Edward M. Almond; Adm. Sherman and Gen. Collins of the J.C.S.; Adm. Arthur W. Radford, Allied Naval Commander in Chief, Pacific; Vice-Adm. A. D. Struble, commanding the 7th Fleet which occupied Japanese waters; and Rear Adm. James H. Doyle who, immediately junior to Struble, would command the projected amphibious operation for which he had gained much experience in the Pacific. MacArthur was always conscious of the parallel between his operation and Wolfe's at Quebec, in which case Doyle was to Smith as Saunders had been to Wolfe. MacArthur himself held a more elevated position than even Wolfe. Curiously, neither Shepherd nor Smith was invited to attend the conference.

But what were the strategic advantages and disadvantages so eloquently propounded by MacArthur which persuaded President Truman that his veteran soldier's precious lodestone was worthy of support? The disadvantages were always evident. "We drew up a list of every conceivable and natural handicap and Inchon had 'em all," said Lt. Cmdr. Arlie Capps, Adm. Doyle's Gunfire Support Officer.[3] And yet, almost above all modern amphibious operations, MacArthur needed timing, luck, precise coordination, and, most vitally, the element of surprise. The reader, therefore, is asked to bear the following conflicting elements in mind.

The most serious difficulty at Inchon was its tidal range which varied by 32 feet, second only to the 40-50 foot range in the Bay of Fundy, between New Brunswick and Nova Scotia. On the ebb tide the harbor became a vast mudflat, stretching three miles out to sea, and changing every channel and inlet to coils of twisting mud. Most landing craft had a draft of 29 feet, and thus only on September 15th and 27th and October 11th would the tide be high enough to take them safely into Inchon, so that they could enter and leave port for three hours on each tide. October 11th was clearly too late. But there would only be two hours of full tide on September 15th and 27th. This extraordinary phenomenon was caused by the nature of the entrance to the port, approached from the Yellow Sea through Flying Fish Channel, which has a five-knot current and is studded with rocks, shoals, reefs, and islands which congest the water into a bore and withhold its flow for an unduly long period. For this reason alone only the Japanese, in 1894 and 1904, with shallow-draft vessels, had taken naval craft into Inchon. But it is certain that no one will do so again.

But as a result of the tide there was another insuperable difficulty, that of the mudflats which, presenting a barrier of three miles every eight hours, meant that the invasion force could not float in and out, but simply remain like sitting ducks at the mercy of the enemy's artillery. The only answer was massive invasion coverage. The biggest sitting duck of all was the island of Wolmi-do known as Green Beach which not only prevented the Marines from having a clear run at the enemy from the sea, but was the tide's most upsetting factor and the most inconvenient of the studded islets which would require an invasion force of its own, thus inevitably reducing the invasion strength of one of the other beaches. And when the tide receded, one battalion would be perched on the island, linked by a direct causeway with the unknown forces on the mainland.

The word beach was itself a misnomer (except as "litus"), for the whole coastline adjacent to Inchon consisted of fjords and spits of land, immediately overlooked by the forward slopes of precipitous hill features which would ideally suit the defenders. There was no gradual beach on the ideal Normandy pattern and there could be no Dieppe raid anywhere along the coast to test the defenders first. The last of the natural disadvantages was the imminence of the typhoon season, and even as the invasion fleet was making for Inchon, so was Typhoon Jane; while Kezia was mustering her assault from the other side of the Korean peninsula.

MacArthur retorted, in answer to questions from a battery of critics, that "the very arguments you have made as to the impracticabilities involved will tend to ensure for me the element of surprise. For the enemy commander will reason that no one would be so brash as to make such an attempt." This, he said, was the secret of Wolfe's success, for only an apparently insane general would have led his men up the Heights of Abraham; yet such insanity was the secret at St. Nazaire. And optimism cut both ways, for MacArthur discounted the probability of the Chinese ever smashing through the U.N.'s line south of the Yalu by exclaiming that "no commander in his right senses" [4] would attempt such an undertaking in winter. Apart from those mentioned, the disadvantage with which, at the last moment, MacArthur was to have the most severe misgivings was the distance between his invasion and Walker's entrapped Army in the Pusan perimeter. Here morale was miserable, despite the commander's brave efforts to make his men realize the truth of the situation: "There will be no more retreating! . . . We must fight to the end! . . .We are going to hold this line! We are going to win!" [5] But the unfortunate Gen. Walker was desperately short of seasoned officers and men and an interminable series of holding actions had, Mac-Arthur felt, become the Eighth Army's psychological habit. By the time of MacArthur's conference there were about 140,000 United Nations soldiers inside the perimeter, being held by only about 70,000 communists. The Commander in Chief even considered replacing Walker by a man who had not had the General's harsh experience. At one time during the later stages of the Inchon landing, when during the breakout from the beach-head there was still little response from the perimeter, Mac-Arthur so doubted the Eighth Army's psychological ability to smash its constrictors that he seriously considered Collins' idea of launching an offensive at Kunsan, further south and within reach of the entrapped Army, if the trapped men could concert one enormous effort. But Kunsan was advocated instead of Inchon by several of the General's listeners who felt that they had found the suitable compromise between a hare-brained scheme and a total lack of imagination. But, in his heart, each commander knew that Kunsan would ultimately be something of nothing; while Inchon was a daring and noble thrust of arms. Inchon—thereon had MacArthur set his heart!

But if Walker's Army were low in morale, the drainage of his men for MacArthur's apparently lunatic scheme would surely lower it even further. The Commander in Chief was asking the J.C.S. and other senior commanders not only to join him in a reckless gamble but was also apparently seeking to jeopardize further the men at Pusan. For some American generals, like Collins, the memory of Anzio was still sufficiently fresh in their minds to prevent them from regarding *Chromite* with anything but severe anxiety and misgivings. But then MacArthur, or even just an average commander, would never have allowed his men to get stuck at Anzio. But the risk remained; if X Corps failed to hold the beachhead, or was simply pinned down on the beaches for long enough to erode the element of surprise, American (and thereby U.N.) defeat in Korea was certain and the quantity of prisoners which the NKPA could take would give Kim Il-sung immense bargaining power. Lastly there was the logistical problem, for Inchon's harbor facilities could handle only 6,000 tons of equipment at a time, or ten per cent of Pusan's, which itself was regarded as inadequate. Only a man of MacArthur's prestige and self-confidence could talk himself out of all this.

What advantages could there be against these apparently insuperable difficulties? Whatever they were, they were creatures of necessity. David Rees, the author of a fine book on the Korean War (*Korea: The Limited War*), has called Inchon a "Twentieth Century Cannae," and certainly when one weighs up the conception in the abstract one can only compare the undertaking's apparent hopelessness with Hannibal's in 216 B.C. But similarity became irony, for Hannibal's defeat of Scipio turned eventually to withdrawal, and in its turn, the Roman Empire awoke, with this catalyst, to victory. MacArthur would never have guessed what futurity held for him and I doubt whether many historians have seen the comparison with Cannae beyond the elephants, because one doubts really whether the Korean War was ever terminated in any sense. There can be no doubt that Inchon closed the first phase. Daring and brilliant generals, however, are a universal species; whether we are thinking about Genghis Khan, Wellington, or Emilio Mola. But Cannae, or Blenheim for that matter, did not just occur, and we must be quite clear in our own minds, as MacArthur was, about the merits and demerits of *Chromite*. Place yourself, reader, in the General's chair in his spacious office on the sixth floor of the Dai Ichi Building, facing a dozen skeptical commanders and their aides who watch you with incredulity and wonder why you were not replaced at the end of World War II. But as the commanders were to learn, MacArthur had worked out what they had barely even considered and had sought the finest advice—not least their own, unwittingly given.

Strategically, as I have pointed out, Inchon was ideal, both because the enemy would least expect an assault there and because it was close to Seoul. If secured at this point, the route north and south of Seoul would be severed between the main artery from Pyongyang to Pusan. MacArthur's knowledge of the Orient (no doubt he recalled his study of Korea when first he served there in 1905) enabled him to argue with unique authority with his protagonists. He pointed out, almost co-incidentally, a matter which was of immediate importance to the Koreans—that success at Inchon would enable the South Koreans to harvest their rice crop and provide the food with which to substantiate the liberation of Seoul, with its accompanying boost to morale for Syngman's people. Truck loads of rice would accompany the machine guns and mortar bombs. All the General's contentions supported surprise. If, with gigantic support from sea and air, success could be achieved at Inchon, a swift reversal of fortune would be inevitable. But there still remained the whole purpose of the operation and its worrying uncertainty; could Walker manage his part of the strategy? MacArthur was the past master of the amphibious operation, which alone strengthened his hand, and if he could afford it he would beat the enemy before the first Marine stepped ashore and stretch his enemy's technical resources in ever widening directions.

His briefing took 45 minutes before the skeptics broke their enthralled silence. Gen. Ridgway was an early convert, although after the Chinese intervention he became a stern protagonist of the strategy of limited war. He duly recorded in his book that "as for Inchon, the brilliance of his plan, the logic of its conception, and the extreme care with which the finest detail had been dealt with persuaded me quickly to support it. But this was not my decision to make; and before the operation could be approved there were doubting Thomases on the JC.S. who had to be won over." [6] Sherman and Collins had been in Tokyo since the middle of August. *Bluehearts* had soon to be discussed by the resident commanders and one meeting had been held as early as July 4th—an ominous date! Several individual discussions were held before all were gathered together on August 23rd. Adm. Doyle confessed afterwards that "the best I can say is that Inchon is not impossible"; [7] and even Sherman, the most skeptical of those present, was according to Joy, "almost persuaded." [8] Collins disliked having to denude the Pusan perimeter of Marines* and, eventually, of the 7th Infantry Division. As already mentioned, both he and Sherman doubted the wisdom of siting the invason so far north in case of misadventure, when the allies would lose on two fronts. But from the diplomatic point of view Harriman had already confided to Norstad and Ridgway that "political and personal considerations should be put to one side and our government deal with Gen. MacArthur on the lofty level of the great national asset which he is." [9] Even in Tokyo, back on July 13th, when Mac-Arthur confirmed that *Operation Bluehearts* was no longer feasible because the G.I.'s (as opposed to Marines) he needed were too preoccupied in the perimeter and the enemy's advance was too rapid, Collins, fearing that MacArthur was going to over-involve the United States Army from elsewhere in his embryonic plan, had said, "General, you are going to have to win the war out here with the troops available to you in Japan and Korea." [10] According to Adm. Radford, MacArthur shook his head and smiled, "Joe, you are going to have to change your mind." [11] But until the Chinese "volunteers" appeared and the fortunes of the war were reversed, Collins was able by eager Marine intervention to enforce his will. A reduced cadre of the 1st and 5th Marines was the only loss from the southern front. While some service chiefs were reluctant to accede, General Vandenberg evidently felt slighted when he learned that MacArthur's change from *Bluehearts* to *Chromite* involved the exclusive use of the Marines, in the initial stages at least, and the use entirely of their Air Wing for cover. As a gesture of disapproval he sent only a representative to the conference on August 23rd, rather than go himself.

MacArthur concluded his address in histrionic style, "I can almost hear the ticking of the second hand of destiny. We must

* Although they were actually the responsibility of the Chief of Naval Staff.

act now or we will die." Except that he would have used
"perish" as the ultimate word, Churchill might well have said
the same, using the English language in its completeness to
overcome a logistical weakness. How similar was the range of
their respective military imagination! MacArthur reckoned that
the capture of the port would save 100,000 lives. "We shall
land at Inchon and I shall crush them," [12] he ended as his voice
became a muted drawl. Before the two Chiefs of Staff left for
Washington, Sherman is reported to have said in confidence,
"I wish I had that man's confidence." [13]

MacArthur presumed that he would have his way completely; indeed, he had to if *Chromite* were to succeed and the
United Nations forces were to be rescued. The movement and
logistics of various Marine units will be described in due
course. As a mere formality the J.C.S. finally approved the
operation which was already as well rehearsed as possible on
September 8th, only a week before it occurred, because, to their
relief, the buck had passed from them to the President. Thence-
forward Truman would take the ultimate responsibility, for
was it not President Truman himself who kept a famous notice
on his desk in the White House, "The buck stops here!"? But
when his Joint Chiefs of Staff, who were still not entirely
happy about the prospect, reported on the conference in Tokyo
and their subsequent discussions to the President, he saw the
Inchon landing as a separate military entity and, as such, said
that it was "a bold plan worthy of a master strategist." [14] As
such it must remain, irrespective of the disaster that followed.

Before we proceed too far, and certainly before landing with
3/5th Marines on Green Beach, a word must be said about
the parlous state of America's armed forces in 1950, of inter-
service rivalry and of the reciprocal relations which these had
upon the Inchon operation and its projected Marine contingent.
The speed and efficiency with which the Marines were "demoth-
balled" will be apparent. One or two occurrences in the late
forties, during the postwar euphoria, indicate that had it not
been for the Korean War in general and the Inchon landing in
particular, the United States armed forces, particularly the
Marine Corps, would have been allowed to fall to the tempta-
tion of near disbandment, from which re-emergence would have

been a long and difficult process. Only the United States' Rhine Army seemed to demand constant attention.

But just as MacArthur had few allies in high places in 1950 (except, perhaps, the Japanese themselves), so even before the Korean War he had constantly complained to the J.C.S. about the severely reduced manpower he commanded in the Far East. No doubt, America's atomic superiority had made her over-confident, while the J.C.S. had claimed that the despatch of more men to Korea would escalate the war to worldwide proportions which would be unjustified in view of what they believed to be the strategic unimportance of Korea.

From his own point of view MacArthur could argue with evident logic and feel that he had cause for concern. Gen. Walker's Eighth Army, the United States's highest military command in the Far East, based on Tokyo, should have been established at 18,900 men when, in fact, the figure stood at only 12,500. Artillery and armor were correspondingly weak. Little more could be said of the Air Force, while the Marines were virtually non-existent. With this distinguished Corps, Bradley, as he had shown in his speech of October 19, 1949, had never had great sympathy; while at the same time his seniority in the U.S. Army in northwest Europe during the war, just below Eisenhower, had persuaded him that that was the theatre to which prior attention should always be given. After all, the Western powers were still living under the shadow of the recent Berlin Airlift. Bradley was not popular with the Navy and was heartily disliked by the Marines; and to make matters worse he was not greatly concerned with the Far East. That the Chairman of the Joint Chiefs of Staff himself should hold such views will indicate why MacArthur's forces were in such a parlous condition on June 24, 1950, and at the same time emphasize the insistence with which he had to regard the importance of his theatre of command in order to implement *Operation Chromite* successfully less than three months later. It was hard enough to maintain anything approaching normality even in peacetime. Only the disastrous early course of the war, and MacArthur's eloquence and reputation, assisted by a vocal public (which unfortunately over-reacted to the extent of McCarthy's "witch hunts" against perpetrators of "Unamerican

Activities," the zealous prosecution of Alger Hiss, etc.) and a vigilant press, enabled MacArthur to receive the supplies he needed.

Gen. Bradley's pronouncement about the future of amphibious operations was bad enough, but it was with utter incredulity that the U.S. Navy and Marine Corps heard of the remarks of the Secretary of Defense, Louis A. Johnson, to Adm. Richard L. Connolly:

> Admiral, the Navy is on its way out. . . . There's no reason for having a Navy and Marine Corps. General Bradley tells me that amphibious operations are a thing of the past. We'll never have any more amphibious operations. That does away with the Marine Corps. And the Air Force can do anything the Navy can do nowadays, so that does away with the Navy.[15]

The chief result of this naiveté was to sharpen inter-service rivalry. For the Marines, at the bottom of the heap, the situation was desperate, and in an ironic sense there were many servicemen who inwardly welcomed the Korean War as a means of the survival of their prized and particular service. Two men, apart from MacArthur, were pre-eminent in the rescue of the Marine Corps; its unfortunate Commandant, the four-star Gen. Clifton B. Cates, and its Pacific Fleet Commander, Lt. Gen. Lemuel Shepherd, Cates' successor.

As soon as Shepherd heard of the outbreak of war he continued on to Tokyo from the US-Pearl Harbor journey, from which he took up his new Pacific command. He had spoken briefly to Admiral Radford and now had the authority, pending J.C.S. approval, to offer MacArthur at least a Marine Brigade—6,534 strong—which eventually reached Korea on August 2nd and was to be invaluable during the desperate fighting for the Pusan perimeter. Cates had urged him to go all out for this authority.

Cates himself was directly responsible to the Chief of Naval Operations, Adm. Sherman, and, after Johnson's remarks, was anxious to prove the Marines in Korea as a means of their survival. But he always felt that he had a strong ally in Gen. MacArthur who had relied so heavily on the Marines in the

Pacific. As early as June 29th, having unsuccessfully sought an interview with Sherman four days earlier, Cates ran into him in the main hall of the Pentagon. According to Cates the conversation went thus:

> CATES: Things are looking pretty grim over there. Why doesn't MacArthur ask for Marines?
> SHERMAN: (after a pause) What do you have?
> CATES: I can give you an R.C.T. and an Air Group from the west coast.
> SHERMAN: (another pause) Leave it to me. I'll send a "Blue Flag" to Joy.[16]

One can easily picture the scene—the bustling and energetic little Cates and the white-haired, soft-spoken Sherman, well known in the Pentagon for his disarming taciturnity.

This brings us to the second of MacArthur's daunting tasks —to ensure the correct disposition of his Marine units from their scattered theatres of command and the adequate assistance of the fleet and the Marine Air Wing in time to support the invasion which, so the tide determined, would be on September 15th. First, where were the Marines who had so readily made themselves available and thereby eased the Commander in Chief's task? They were arriving fast from every quarter of the globe.

Following Shepherd's offer to MacArthur the latter wasted no time in asking the Pentagon for the two remaining regiments of the 1st Division. These consisted of the 5th Marines, which were sailing between July 12th and July 14th from San Diego to the Pusan perimeter where they would become the 1st Provisional Marine Brigade. In addition, the Division's reserves were also mobilized; but on July 25th, the J.C.S. allowed MacArthur to have only the 1st Marines, eventually changing their minds so that on August 10th they decided to send the 7th as well. MacArthur's persuasion of his nominally superior officers to throw in the 5th Marines resulted from the high point of his advocacy. Being the world's most senior active general officer inevitably carried weight. Thus he would officially be allowed to have the whole division for *Operation Chromite*, but for D-Day itself he could commit only two regiments to action at Inchon, the 1st and the 5th Marines * which would now be his to do as he considered best. From Camp Pendleton and San Diego embarkation got under way with great speed and enthusiasm between the end of July and the middle of August, when Smith himself left for Tokyo, en route to assume command of the Division. The 7th Marines were eventually committed to action at Seoul as a hybrid unit of the Marine Corps' eager but rather less efficiently trained members. At this time, however, they were seven thousand miles away, training with the Sixth Fleet in the Mediterranean; but they were eventually ordered east, via Suez and Ceylon, on August 16th.

Meanwhile, *Chromite* was being planned down to its minutest detail by the Inter-Services' Joint Strategic Plans and Operations Group of Far East Command. Almond† was appointed to command X Corps, the senior operational unit at Inchon, on August 26th; and under him the various commanders and staff officers were given their respective responsibilities. That MacArthur should appoint his own Chief of Staff to command X Corps was initially seen by him as a means of facilitating the operation, since Almond was, in any case, the general most privy to the Commander in Chief's plans and intentions; it indicates how quickly MacArthur expected the operation to achieve its purpose. Mention has been made elsewhere, however, of the unsuitability of a soldier's commanding what was essentially a Marine venture, as Almond did, and he was regarded with a certain disfavor by the senior Marines. Apart from the 1st Marine Division, used throughout, and what could be procured of the South Korean Marine Corps, the remaining division was the 7th Infantry, commanded by Maj. Gen. David G. Barr. These were the only troops sent straight to Inchon from Tokyo.

But by the time Inchon had been assaulted Britain also had forces in the field, helping to hold the western flank of the Pusan perimeter. These consisted chiefly of the 1st Middlesex

---

* Excluding the 11th Marines (Artillery).

† Almond was an Army officer who had originally failed to be commissioned in the Marine Corps. He had experienced both world wars and was much decorated.

Regiment, the 1st Argyll and Sutherland Highlanders, and full brigade support of artillery, RE and other arms, all under the command of Brig. Basil Coad, DSO. Soon this would become the 27th Brigade and eventually the Commonwealth Division, to which Britain sent two brigades. If this seems a relatively small contribution it should be remembered that an essentially national service army was having to man trouble spots all over the world, in the crumbling Empire, North Africa, and the Canal Zone, and in Germany and the British Sector of Berlin. Acrimony between Britain and the U.S. had existed virtually as a result of America's embarrassing retreat before the supposed nonentities from North Korea.

On July 26, 1950 Emanuel Shinwell, the Secretary of State for Defense, told the House of Commons that a further £100 million would be devoted to defense spending; but that nothing new would come into effect until after the summer recess. The Opposition was scandalized by the procrastination, so that Churchill, Eden, and Clement Davies, the Liberal leader, made an urgent request to see Attlee and his Foreign Secretary, Ernest Bevin. But the Government was unmoved and the Prime Minister explained to the King that he would not betray the appearance of a constitutionally elected administration being bullied by the official opposition, and on August 17th the Speaker made it clear that he would not order the House back. It had risen on August 5th but three days later the Government agreed in principle to an increase of £3,400 million over 3 years, a rise of about 9% of the national revenue. National Service was forthwith increased from 18 months to two years and alterations were made to Britain's logistical situation. But the Government would not be coerced by the Opposition.

Inchon relieved the immediate problem, for with success there was less internecine acrimony; but other problems were created in the wake of MacArthur's subsequent retreat. The United States looked around for a whipping boy, and so accused Britain of contributing too little to the war effort, and while Bevin concurred with MacArthur's conduct of the war as being in order with Britain's requirement, Shinwell told an audience in Durham on December 3rd that the Commander in Chief had exceeded his terms of reference. Furthermore, the British

Government felt that the United States was courting wholesale war by the degree of her aggression towards Red China when she should have been considering the power of the Sino-Soviet axis. The United States felt that Britain was aiding an alien against an ally when, despite Nationalist China, she had recognized Mao Tse-tung's communist regime on January 6, 1950.

On the same day that Shinwell was speaking in Durham the Prime Minister set out for Washington to disabuse his allies of their misgivings about Britain. He was only partially successful when he wanted full understanding, if only for the good political reason that the Labour Party, halfway through its last brief term of office, needed to show that there was no weakening in the allegiance of Britain with America. But Attlee had already explained to the House of Commons that Article 51 of the United Nations Charter did not prevent Britain's allegiance with the United States in Korea, under the auspices of the United Nations. He was soon able, therefore, to dispel the absurd idea which had developed in the United States that Britain intended to withdraw her forces from the war. But Attlee could not persuade Truman to see the danger in regarding China with such abandoned belligerence. All this surely puts the relation between Truman and MacArthur into greater perspective and indicates a consideration the President must have had in making up his mind about the dismissal.

That Attlee was placed in a most unenviable position can be seen by the discord within his own government during its swan song. On the one hand he had to convince the United States that he was sending adequate reinforcements to fight for the United Nations and on the other he had to marshal his left wing in the name of party solidarity. But the latter had had enough and in the face of the Defense estimates of 1951 three ministers resigned; the most serious defector was Aneurin Bevan, Minister of Health and castigator of expense upon armaments; in addition there was the young Harold Wilson, President of the Board of Trade, and John Freeman, Parliamentary Secretary to the Ministry of Supply and a future Ambassador to the United States. But the position became a little more diplomatically accommodating when Churchill's Conservative Government was returned to power in the autumn of 1951 and the traditionally higher values were placed by the Tories on Defense.

Although this may take us beyond the immediate concern of *Chromite* it illustrates the point that whereas the commander needs to be concerned only with his strategy, his Government and its military advisors have to weigh circumstances seen and unseen. So back from other considerations specifically to Inchon and the circumstances which at a casual glance would seem to dominate the war. MacArthur had acquired his invasion troops. The matter of who was going to command what among the Marines, jealously guarding their own responsibilities, was naturally left to Shepherd and particularly Smith. The command of the 5th Marines went not to a full colonel, but to Lt. Col. Raymond L. Murray in whom Smith had particular confidence. The man who was to lead the 1st Marines was an old warrior with almost fanatical devotion to the Marine Corps. He was Col. Lewis B. (Chesty) Puller who had spent $19 worth of telegrams to Gen. Cates, eagerly volunteering his services to come out of retirement, mobilize the Regiment and prove his worth in Korea, a request to which Cates conceded.

Adm. Struble, commanding the 7th Fleet, led the allied warships in Far Eastern waters and was responsible for the liaison of all the vessels and landing craft as they assembled in various ports, before uniting their armada towards Inchon where the naval responsibility for the landing would be handed over to Rear Adm. Doyle. Struble's entire fleet consisted of 260 vessels, carrying nearly 70,000 men, and including ships from the United States, Britain, Australia, Canada, New Zealand, France, and Holland. Among Britain's warships was the escort carrier, HMS *Triumph*, while its flagship was HMS *Belfast*, now a floating museum in the Pool of London; but for the actual bombardment the flag of Rear Adm. Andrewes was flown from HMS *Jamaica* which, with HMS *Kenya*, pounded Blue Beach. Only MacArthur could have taken responsibility for the fact that there were 37 Japanese-manned LST's. The Marine Division assembled at Kobe, the 5th Regiment having come from Pusan and the 7th from Yokohama. Struble's flagship was the heavy cruiser, USS *Rochester*; while Doyle's flagship, the USS *Mount McKinley*, in effect became the most important ship in the fleet because it would be most directly concerned with the landing and carried most of the senior Marine officers including Gen. MacArthur himself.* The Gunfire Support Group was commanded by Rear Adm. John M. Higgins whose flagship was the cruiser, USS *Toledo*. Vital to the whole undertaking were the aircraft carriers, the most important of which were those in Rear Adm. Edward C. Ewen's Fast Carrier Force 77. Adm. Andrewes commanded the Blockade and Covering Force.

Preceded by the Support Group the *Mount McKinley* cast off from Sasebo on September 13th—D-Day minus 2. All had gone without a hitch. The only assailant so far was the weather for on September 11th, as the fleet was sailing up the Yellow Sea, Typhoon Kezia struck from the Pacific with winds up to 125 mph.

---

* MacArthur was criticized for placing himself, the X Corps Commander, and all his senior staff officers in the same vessel.

CHAPTER THREE

Green Beach and the Seizure of Wolmi-do

Even such a surprise assault as that at Inchon had to have adequate military support both from the sea and the air; indeed, probably more so than others. It has been the case with every amphibious operation in recent times. The problem is to know how to maximize the support while at the same time to minimize the warning. The traditional answer is that while the landing zone must be sufficiently supported, other areas must also be pounded in order to deceive the enemy for as long and as late as possible. This was the answer at Inchon, no less than for the invasion of Normandy or New Guinea. And yet MacArthur's security was one of the less successful aspects of Inchon, as Adm. Andrewes later wrote:

Security was sadly lacking. . . . I do not believe, however, that such a plan could possibly have been produced and put into operation so quickly had not a huge army of people worked at it, and there is no doubt that in one respect the enemy must have been completely wrong. He cannot possibly have guessed at the strength of the blow. That had to be seen to be believed.[1]

And so, on first-hand evidence and despite difficulties with the J.C.S., MacArthur eventually managed to pack an enormous punch which more than compensated for his lack of security. The Press Club in Tokyo had even called *Chromite* "Operation Common Knowledge." But, secure or not, the U.N. correctly assumed that the communists would not believe their enemy to be so lunatic, or else the NKPA were uncharacteristically slow-witted.

The strategy of diversifying the assault to confuse the enemy was used particularly by the U.S. Marine Air Wing, under the command of Gens. Cushman and Harris, in conjunction with the British Fleet Air Arm, over all parts of Korea. The road, railway, and supply routes and the power station between Wonsan on the east coast and the 38th parallel were hit hard, and initially the North Koreans must have regarded this as a likely beachhead. But then Seoul, Haeju, Pyongyang, Kaesong, and Kunchon were truly plastered. Scarcely had these targets been hit than Wolmi-do received 42 sorties and Inchon itself 36. When Lt. D. H. Cole climbed out of his Corsair onto the flight deck of the aircraft carrier, the USS *Valley Forge*, the United States had completed her 10,000th sortie of the war. By now the enemy must have known that they were under U.N. threat of another kind altogether, and that this was not simply assistance for the Eighth Army; but where, when, and of what strength? They were soon to discover.

Because they were the first uninvited visitors, the Marine Air Wing's attack should be described before we move on to the naval bombardment. The intensive softening up operations began on September 10th (D-Day—5), and continued with increasing ferocity until by D—2 all escort carriers were in the area of Inchon. The U.N. had complete command of the air and sea, and every available Corsair of both Marine squadrons was armed with double loads of napalm*—two 150-gallon tanks per plane, 95,000 pounds in all, with their assigned target the wooden roofed island of Wolmi-do. Meanwhile, Task Force 77 sealed off the Inchon-Seoul objective area, and the new Panther jets struck at every known enemy airfield in the area as a precautionary measure. Even on D—1 the Air Wing and Fleet Air Arm maintained thrusts, apparently from Japan, to sustain surprise for as long as possible. As a final *coup de grace* Ewen's force hit Inchon and Kimpo airfields with his mighty A.D.'s, the Douglas Skyraiders and the heaviest bomb carriers avail-

---

* Napalm was first used in Korea on June 30, 1950, from jettisonable fuel tanks mounted under aircraft wings.

able to the Marines, which were still in service in Vietnam 17 years later.

MacArthur had hit his enemy unaware; but while he still tried, perhaps rather clumsily, to maintain secrecy as to the precise area of his landing there could be no doubt that he had paved the way for a sinister new thrust. Perhaps the least credible of his feints and deceptions was carried out on the night of September 12–13th, when he tried to maintain the illusion of an assault on Kunsan by implementing a landing from HMS *Whitesand Bay* within the U.S. Special Operations Company, under Col. Louis B. Ely, and a unit of the 41st Royal Marine Commando under Lt. E. G. D. Pounds. As a result of the rather confused fighting which followed three American Marines were killed. In view of this force's assignment these losses conjure up a rather tragic notion—a prearranged wastage, however strategically justifiable.

While the last diversionary raids were being made, and at the same time the target area was being bombed with napalm, the fleet was making its way northward towards Flying Fish Channel where it would take station and then, moving to its allotted positions, begin the naval bombardment from the sea. Already ships of the Royal Navy had shelled Wolmi-do on September 5–6th from the northern approaches to Flying Fish Channel in order to tempt the enemy to lay mines in those waters, under the false impression that that was the direction from which the invaders would approach the harbor, if at all. But at 0700 hours on September 13th, D-2, the North Koreans could have been in no doubt, for then the cruisers and destroyers nosed their way into the channel from a southern direction, just north of the island of Yonghungdo (which name is not to be confused with Yongdungpo). But already Struble had experienced the very obstacle which, in these narrow waters, he most dreaded—mines. Enemy craft had actually been encountered laying the things on September 10th, and four more mines were spotted on September 13th, but successfully detonated by 40-mm rounds from the destroyers.* All ships'

---

* Such military stratagems are now as obsolete as the bowmen of Agincourt.

radios were silent as the USS *Rochester* steamed slowly through the barely dawn-lit sea. She was joined by the *Toledo* and astern of them were the British light cruisers, *Jamaica* and *Kenya*. Ahead were some of Commodore Allen's destroyers (90), Capt. Sears' Advance Attach Group (90.1) which included his flagship, the *Mansfield*, and the *De Haven, Swenson, Collett,* and *Henderson*. Lastly, among the destroyers, came the *Gurke* which, approaching from the west, closed on the *Toledo*'s starboard beam and managed to attach a line with a pouch which contained the last aerial photographs from aircraft of the *Valley Forge*, flagship of Ewen's fast carriers.

At 1242 hours the USS *Gurke* dropped anchor three miles north of Wolmi-do and the others followed; the *De Haven*'s 5-in. guns made first move and battle commenced at 1255 hours. The destroyers ripped close inshore at about 25 knots before, at 1347, Allen ordered retirement. The *De Haven* had fired 998 rounds, but despite the aerial sorties the ships had found the North Korean 918th Coastal Battery still very much alive, if rather inaccurate. The only fatal casualty in the U.S. fleet, ironically enough, was Lt. David H. Swenson who was killed on the bridge of the very ship named after his uncle, a captain of renown in the South Pacific during the Second World War. Next morning, when the destroyers revisited the waters off Wolmi-do, they found the coastal battery curiously silent. But they poured in at least another 1,700 5-in. shells, meeting only scattered resistance, thanks largely to aircraft of the carriers VMF-214 and -323 which, having returned from Sasebo, were busy spotting for the cruisers and launching napalm strikes before and after the big ships' bombardment.

The cruisers had had an unusual experience, for as they had ridden at anchor well offshore on September 13th they watched the reaction of the destroyers to a signal which had been given by the ever vigilant Higgins in this most extraordinary of amphibious operations. The possibility of enemy small craft loaded with infantry taking advantage of the receding tide and expanding mudflats had not escaped him and he gave the historic order, "Prepare to repel all boarders!" The crew of the fleet duly armed themselves with grenades and machine guns and watched through the dusky murk for sign of an enemy who did not appear. At 1116 hours on D-1 it was the cruisers' turn, and the *Rochester, Toledo, Jamaica*, and *Kenya* opened up with their 8-in. and 6-in. guns from the close proximity of 800 yards before the honors passed back again to the destroyers. Their 1,732-shell salvo, previously mentioned, was only marginally less than the 5-in. shelling which had hit Omaha Beach on D-Day in 1944. According to an aerial observer, Wolmi-do was just "one worthless piece of real estate."

Now all was ready for Act 1, scene 2, which was the capture of Green Beach. At midnight on September 14–15th the fleet took up its station again at the entrance to Flying Fish Channel; at 0254 hours on D-Day Sears' A.A.G. 90.1 glided past; at 0454 the first aircraft orbited the invasion area; at 0520 the signal was hoisted to the yardarm of the *Mount McKinley*, "Land the Landing Force"; at 0545 the cruisers opened fire; at 0600 the landing force took to the boats; between 0600 and 0615 Marine Corsairs gave the target area a final solo aerial bombardment; at 0615 the destroyers and LST's completed their gunnery missions and at 0633 hours, three minutes late, the 3rd Battalion of the 5th Marines landed on Wolmi-do. Meanwhile, at first light, the *Mount McKinley* had entered the channel and the Commander in Chief was up early and waiting eagerly in the Admiral's swivel chair with his binoculars to watch the curtain go up on scene 2.

But these facts are merely the skeleton of the pre-invasion schedule. On D-Day-1, as the *Mount McKinley* was steaming up the Yellow Sea, MacArthur was in an euphoric mood. While he and his commanders enjoyed a lavish lunch, followed by cigars, he regaled the company with memories of old battles and clearly enjoyed the enraptured attention which he received from his devoted staff. Only Gen. Smith, as he remarked in his diary, found the occasion rather boring, no doubt because he and Doyle would bear the most responsibility for events next day. Then after lunch, with that same profound self-confidence which Wellington had shown on the eve of Waterloo and Montgomery before El Alamein, MacArthur retired for his afternoon's siesta.

At about the moment when the General awoke there appeared from the bridge of the USS LSMR-401 a mere bombardment rocket ship of the kind which was to be so invaluable at Inchon, a large formation of smoke looming high beyond the horizon, "dead on the bearing of Inchon, 65 miles ahead. Cmdr. Clarence T. Doss, Jr., commander of the three rocket ships, had word passed to all hands. The pillar of smoke spoke for itself. 'It was welcome news,' said Doss." [2]

Night fell. The sun would rise upon that phenomenon of even the best conducted operatons—chaos, perhaps even agony and an experience which would give the beginner such hell on earth as he could never have thought existed. But chaos is relative and courage always comes from unexpected sources. The night, commented Capt. Sears, was "as dark as the inside of a cow's belly." But as the sun rose Wolmi-do, or Green Beach, would be assaulted by the 5th Marines' 3rd Battalion, under the command of Lt. Col. Robert D. Taplett. Briefly, the deployment was as follows: three light transports and an LSD would carry the advance group who would be crammed at twice the normal capacity. The two assault companies, the experienced G and H, were in the destroyers USS *Diachenko* and *Horace A. Bass* respectively, while Taplett's I Company would land in reserve from the destroyer USS *Wantuck*. Meanwhile, the tanks, vehicles, and other heavy equipment would be under the eye of Battalion H.Q. in Capt. Sears' flagship, the LSD *Fort Marion*.

At midnight the naval force proceeded to its station at the entrance to Flying Fish Channel. In the van of the 19-ship column was Allen's destroyer division—*Mansfield, De Haven,* and *Swenson*. Next came Sears' Advance Group which would be particularly concerned with Green Beach—the *Diachenko, Fort Marion, Wantuck,* and *H.A. Bass*. Astern of them, to cover the assault, were Doss' rocket ships—LSMR-401, -403 and -404—vital vessels to the modern navy, but so humble that mere numbers would have to suffice for their nomenclature. Such were the vessels which would be needed immediately. The Second Destroyer Division (90.2) under Allen's overall Destroyer Command which, generally speaking, would be more involved with Red Beach, consisted of the USS *Southerland, Gurke,* and *Henderson*. Immediately astern of them, about three-quarters of the way down the line, was Adm. Doyle's flagship, *Rochester*, centrally placed behind the *Mount McKin-ley*, and astern of them, were the British light cruisers, *Jamaica* and *Kenya*.

When at 0254 hours Sears' destroyers and the three LSMR's moved up to take their position closer inshore to support the landing, the four cruisers trained their guns on Inchon's port installations. But the fleet had had unexpected good fortune as a result of the courage and initiative of a single officer. Several marines had been landed at various points along the coast adjacent to Inchon to report on the country and the enemy's dispositions. Notable among these was a young attached naval lieutenant, Eugene Clark, who had been landed on September 1st to undertake several tasks. The planners wanted to know rather more about the tide, and particularly the effect it had upon the nature of Inchon and Wolmi-do at various stages of its ebb and flow. The position of the enemy's fortification and the regularity of the use of the port for North Korean shipping, civil and military, was also sought. Clark's chief task was to measure the height of the sea wall on Red Beach at high tide. He discovered all this essential information, but also threw in a bonanza. This unscheduled achievement was to climb up and switch on the lighthouse on the tiny island of Palmi-do, at the northern tip of Wolmi-do, in order to guide the fleet on to the targets. As the cruisers waited to cover the destroyers, navigators were peering at their radar screens and lookouts were scanning the horizon. They were more puzzled than ever, therefore, by what they saw. Every 40 seconds the lighthouse beam rotated, and although no one yet knew who was responsible for this blessing all navigators immediately realized their precise positions. Clark, who received the Navy Cross, must remain one of the heroes of Inchon; while Mac-Arthur, who retired late to his cabin, must have been amazed by the sight and reassured of his own infallibility. So much for *Operation Trudy Jackson*.

At 0454 hours Corsairs from Ewen's carriers flashed up from the decks of the *Valley Forge, Philippine Sea*, and *Boxer* which, despite a broken reduction gear, had made three trans-Pacific runs since the beginning of the Korean War with vital supplies of aircraft and ammunition from California and even

Norfolk Island. Recording speeds of over 26 knots the *Boxer* would have held the blue riband of the Pacific, if such had existed. The aircraft orbited the landing area, and those from the *Sicily* and the *Badoeng Strait*, particularly, gave Wolmi-do a further pre-invasion scorch-up.

At 0520 hours Capt. Sears, leading the naval support for Green Beach, began the tortuous procedure that has its roots deep in naval history and the sight of which must have struck mild apprehension through the mind of every amphibious veteran. He signalled to Adm. Doyle that all was ready and the Admiral broke the traditional signal from the yardarm of the *Mount McKinley*, "Land the Landing Force." The Marine craft immediately began embarkation, the chaplains wished God's blessing on each man as he filed past from his respective destroyer or LSD, and with a splash that sent up cavernous bow waves each landing craft hit the water. The punctilious diarist, Gen. Shepherd, wrote: "It was a beautiful morning, and as the first pink streaks of dawn broke in the east my thoughts went back to other dawns when I had watched the preparation to similar landings. . . ." Ten minutes later the ships opened fire, first the destroyers and then the cruisers with their 6- and 8-in. guns, and the diarist continued, "I have never seen any better shooting. . . . The entire island was smothered with bursting shells from the cruisers and destroyers." The bombardment by these ships was joined by that of the rocket ships, the LSMR's -401, -403 and -404.

Now, for the first time, as the sun rose straight ahead of them, the marines saw the target itself silhouetted against the green dawn sky. But to encourage the men as they watched this threatening sight, although it was burning fiercely from its nocturnal blasting, the Corsairs paid the target their last pre-invasion visit, depositing napalm and high explosives on every remaining installation which might still present some threat to the Marines. At 0615, after a quarter of an hour, they returned to the carriers, and the destroyers and rocket ships took over once again. Two of the latter, lying off Red Beach to the north, each fired a thousand 5-in. rockets on the rear eastward coast of Wolmi-do to begin the operation of sealing off those enemy who still imagined that they could escape to the mainland along the causeway which, about a thousand yards long, joined northern Wolmi-do to Inchon. The third rocket ship, LSMR-403, bombarded Green Beach and the high ground to the right while battling against a three-knot current, before taking station for a special operation which I shall describe in due course. It was all evidence of how minutely everything had been planned.

The Marine waves were meanwhile placing themselves in their LCVP's in the rendezvous area, less than a mile off Green Beach. Wave commanders watched the control vessel intently while its red and white flag flew "at the dip." In 15 minutes the first wave would hit the beach, and a reflective silence hung over each craft load as it bobbed up and down on the water. The nervous jokes, which had helped to sustain the morale of youngsters new to war, were over. "Now it's for real!," they pondered on the elusively obvious as they gazed at the brightening sky and the high steel wall of the landing craft. One's inside feels hollow. The final moments took their course. The flag on the control vessel rose to the yardarm and the leading waves—vessels carrying the assault fire teams for G and H Companies, 5th Marines—duly formed up. Over on the port side a rocket ship was pouring its last salvos of 40-mm shells into Green Beach to support the landing, now only two minutes away. Then the flag went down and the coxwains steered the first seven craft at full speed towards the beach. Suddenly, from seaward, came 38 Corsairs to give the landing zone a final work-over. From the sea itself four destroyers and the LSMR-403, now clear of the boat lane, sustained the bombardment. Radio Hill, the pinnacle of the island, seemed to vanish; while Inchon itself was lost behind a haze of hideous ochre smoke and the forward slope of Observatory Hill, the chief feature on the mainland from which resistance might have been expected, looked like nothing the young Marines had ever seen before. The leading craft ground to a halt on the shoaling beach. At 0633 hours the bow ramps dropped open with callous procedure, and the officers and men burst ashore. Two minutes later the second wave of landing craft halted on the steep shoal, and deposited the rest of both companies. The party had begun "for real."

The scene that confronted the Marines on Green Beach was of a low seawall backed by a ridge and, over to their right, a charred hillside, still burning and warm with the shelling it had received. The intense heat, evident as they landed, was wiped away only by the wind which teased the smoke as it rose and coiled from the burning earth. Suddenly, after days of being cooped up in warships and landing craft the Marines found themselves uncomfortably exposed in an alien landscape where, for some unaccountable reason, they expected the enemy to have survived. But the men were prevented from feeling that sudden and chilling exposure to their hidden foes too soon because, as they plunged ashore, Corsairs cleared a swath 50 yards ahead of them, putting down an impregnable curtain of machine gun fire before the defenders could raise their heads. Never in history has such a localized amphibious landing been supported on such a scale. Unlike the broad sweep of the Normandy beach, Wolmi-do was picked out with a needle of pain.

But every man knew his immediate assigned task. They had been over it on maps and rough sand-scale models again and again in the short time since their release from Pusan. All the way up the Yellow Sea they had been told what to do. The Company Commander of the leading assault, G Company, stepped eagerly off the ramp and into the sea over head height. Re-emerging, he wheeled his company to the right and charged straight up the northern slopes of Radio Hill towards the initial beachhead position, known as the 1-A Line. In the van of this advance was 2nd Lt. John D. Counselman whose objective was the summit of Radio Hill. Meanwhile, like released springs, came two other platoons, commanded by Lt. Lawrence O'Connell and Lt. Roger W. Peard, Jr., who prepared to advance southward along the west shore of the island and cut off the causeway leading to a southern exrtemity, So Wolmi-do (Little Moontip Island). But so far enemy resistance was negligible. Above all could be heard the continuous rat-tat-tat of the supporting Corsairs. The only difficulty encountered was caused by the local fishermen whose boats congested the beach so that the Marines had to pour through a gap no more than 50 yards wide. On the left was H Company, which had been detached under Capt. Patrick D. Wildman to clear North

Point. They swung left and across Wolmi-do to the Inchon causeway, and in so doing secured the tactical objective, Line 2-B, which included the eastern end of Radio Hill and the shoreline industrial area opposite Inchon. Already the cruisers had put down considerable firepower on the causeway to cut off the retreating NKPA; but now the Marines were on the spot, the riflemen moving through the industrial district and the engineers laying anti-tank mines at the base of the causeway to prevent a communist counterattack breaking back again. At 0646 the third wave squeezed ashore and disgorged the armored detachments of A Company, among which was the 1st Tank Battalion of ten tanks (2nd Lt. G. W. Sweet), including six M-26 Pershings, one flame thrower, two bulldozers and one tank retriever. No sooner had Lt. Col. Taplett himself come ashore at 0650 than the guide to 3 platoon, Sgt. Alvin E. Smith, planted the flag on to a shell-torn tree on the summit of Radio Hill.

It was not until the main portion of Wolmi-do was supposed to be clear of the enemy that the first resistance took place. Landing in the fourth wave at 0659 hours, Capt. Robert A. McMullen's I Company advanced through North Point in the wake of H Company when they were met by grenade-throwing NKPA of about platoon strength. Well entrenched, the enemy ignored orders to surrender. Behind them came sporadic rifle fire from communist infantrymen concealed in conveniently placed bunkers. The Marines' reaction to this refusal was not pleasant. The Pershings and 'dozers were called up in support, and while Marine riflemen kept the grenadiers' heads down, the bulldozers shovelled the enemy's emplacements over the defenders and the Pershings, working from cave to cave, fired into them at point-blank range. A few stunned, deafened, and bleeding prisoners were duly flushed out. Communist armor which, suddenly appearing from nowhere, tried to detonate the Marines' new minefield was similarly destroyed by the powerful T-26's.

Within an hour of landing on Green Beach the 3/5th Marines controlled over half of Wolmi-do. Only the southern end still remained in the defenders' hands, and while H Company moved beyond the causeway to clear the ruins of the old Esso refinery and the other industrial complex, Taplett reported to the *Mount McKinley*, "Captured 45 prisoners, meeting light resistance." The 105-meter Radio Hill was almost entirely in 1st Lt. L. Bohn's [3] hands and he completed the task simply by sending a force across to the eastern spur and clearing the western reaches of the high ground. By 0800 hours Radio Hill was completely clear, so that all except the promontory of So Wolmi-do had fallen to the Americans in an hour-and-a-half. The *Mount McKinley* was duly informed.

The Commander in Chief immediately cabled Washington, and with the resumption of naval gunfire to support the main assaults on Red and Blue Beaches, MacArthur surveyed the scene from the Admiral's chair. Everyone on Doyle's ship was ecstatic. "Just like Lingayen Gulf," the General told Shepherd, referring to his strategic masterpiece in the Philippines. Shepherd recorded in his diary:

> His staff were grouped around him. He was seated in the Admiral's chair with his old Bataan cap with its tarnished gold braid and a leather jacket on. Photographers were busily engaged in taking pictures of the General while he continued to watch the naval gunfire—paying no attention to his admirers.[4]

MacArthur asked for details of casualties and was told that perhaps a dozen Marines had been killed and that 15 or 20 were wounded, while 45 enemy prisoners had been taken. The General made light of the deaths: "More people get killed in traffic every day." And then came the remark that has always been so prized by those servicemen whom Louis Johnson was keen to demobilize permanently. Turning to Adm. Doyle, MacArthur said, perhaps in rather self-consciously Nelsonian style: "Say to the Fleet, 'The Navy and Marines have never shone more brightly than this morning'." [5] And smiling broadly at his colleagues he said with peerless self-confidence: "That's it. Let's get a cup of coffee."

But it was not quite "it," for the capture of the island's southern tail, the causeway and the island of *So Wolmi-do*, presented an unexpected obstacle. The causeway was about 750 yards long and 12 yards wide, and the small knot of land below it was 500 square yards, topped by a low hill and a navigational beacon. Oblivious of the resistance he would meet here, Taplett redeployed his companies. Three of them immediately faced Inchon, I Company on the North Point, Wildman's H Company on the slopes of Radio Hill, above the industrial area, and G Company on the crest of Radio Hill. Mopping up revealed how well Wolmi-do had been defended before the savage bombardment had torn the defense to shreds. Without it the Marines would, indeed, have been pinned down, Anzio-style. A quick reconnaissance showed how invaluable had been the last-minute close inshore rocket attack of LSMR-403. A one-time swimming pool at North Point (one of the few recognizable pieces of architecture) was now used as a stockade for prisoners of war. The invaders were surprised to find that only along the west coast, at the base of Radio Hill, had mines been laid. U.S. military technology lived up to its superb reputation; medical corpsmen were able to get the wounded across a specially made pier over the mudflats—the lighter casualties to the *Fort Marion* and the seriously wounded to the *Mount McKinley* where they were visited at once by General MacArthur.

Now for Taplett's surprise on "Little Moon-Tip Island" which he commanded to be seized before 1000 hours. Bohn was given an infantry squad, reinforced with a machine gun, commanded by Counselman of 3 platoon, G Company. At the other end of the causeway the NKPA was waiting for them in well-entrenched positions. After a protracted and indecisive exchange of rifle and machine gun fire, Taplett ordered up a tank-infantry team to pin the enemy down while he called for a Marine air mission. A few minutes later Corsairs of VMF-214 burnt up the enemy with napalm, and the end of the causeway was occupied at 1048 hours. Supported by tanks, the main fighting was over by 1115 hours and the mopping up went on for another hour. But the NKPA on *So Wolmi-do* had startled what was swiftly becoming an over-confident invasion force. In this last encounter on Wolmi-do (not that there had been many) 19 enemy surrendered and 17 were killed, including several brave men who had tried to swim to the mainland. Three more marines were wounded at *So Wolmi-do*, which brought the U.S. casualties up to 17 wounded. Taplett's men had taken 136 prisoners and had killed 108 NKPA. Since, according to MacArthur's reconnaissance team, the original number of enemy defenders was about 400, it was estimated that 150 lay entombed in their sealed emplacements. By noon the Marines could content themselves that they were in sole command of the island; but an hour later the tide went out, leaving the 3/5th perched on a piece of muddy "real estate" and watching the mainland anxiously for sign of a counter-attack from all the ideal concealments which remained un-nervingly quiet.

Seoul's two million inhabitants* had been thrown into a state of great excitement, and the NKPA into panic, when they learned that war was again at their front door, or should one say side door? But, like a boxer who has just received a power-ful right jab, the enemy had but a split second to realize that he was about to be struck by a left hook. But it was to be the upper cut that eventually put him on the canvas. What I have called the left hook landed on what MacArthur called Red Beach. North of the point where the Wolmi-do causeway reached Inchon, Red Beach was the northern prong which aimed at the rear of the city's industrial area and the railway to Seoul. So now, to the left hook.

* Seoul was then, as now, the fifth city of Asia.

CHAPTER FOUR

Red Beach and Observatory Hill

The left hook hit Red Beach which lay along about 500 yards of coast from a point immediately north of the junction of the Wolmi-do causeway with Inchon. Only from North Point could the whole of Red Beach be seen by the dawn invaders, as the coast rounded away towards the northeast and the port's dry dock. Thus from the smooth northeastern shore of the island support was available for Red Beach, and the Marines on northern Wolmi-do watched the intense activity throughout the warm afternoon of September 15th; for the assaults on Red Beach and Blue Beach, the latter nearly four miles south of the island and spread over a wide beachhead, were both scheduled for 1730 hours. That MacArthur should compound his difficulties with the rare plan of an evening invasion indicated his utter confidence in *Chromite*, further endorsed by the Marines' outstanding success on Green Beach. Col. Taplett's offer of more than mere covering fire on to Red Beach was declined by Murray.

So close was the new beach that some of Taplett's men under Capt. McMullen, watching the mainland from the north, were sure that they could see mortars and artillery pieces being brought across country; but, if so, they were not used. As we shall see, the 3/5th Marines would eventually rejoin its parent unit, but usually as a reserve battalion, until they all came to the great thrust across the Han which no one imagined would be easily achieved.

Red Beach, to be won by the 1st and 2nd Battalions of the

5th Marines, was the most important inasmuch as it would most closely occupy the main port area of Inchon itself. It had the advantage of support from the 3/5th Marines, firmly established on Wolmi-do, who could cover their comrades from an isolated and entirely occupied position; but the disadvantages of being reduced by one battalion and of having to land on a shore line immediately overlooked by three hill features— Cemetery Hill on its left, the towering Observatory Hill, on the right-center, and the smaller British Consulate Hill, below it on the waterfront. First, I shall describe the strategy which would be adopted, before returning again to the naval and aerial bombardment which would be markedly similar to that already employed on Green Beach. Red Beach was already well bombarded, as peripheral to the earlier target; but Blue Beach, well to the south, would need an entirely separate shelling as Marines at Red and Blue landed simultaneously.

Clark's reconnaissance had established that even at high tide, scaling ladders would be needed to cross the harbor wall on to Red Beach. The primary task of the 5th Marines was to seize the O-1 Line, the initial phase line which was a 3,000-yard arc encompassing the two hills in the left and center, and extending over the last thousand yards through the heavily built-up area back to the coast at the Inner Tidal Basin. The battalions would land in column of companies, on the left of which would be those of Lt. Col. George R. Newton's 1st Battalion which would seize Cemetery Hill and the northern half of Observatory Hill, and on the right those of Lt. Col. Harold S. Roise's 2nd Battalion which would take the rest of Observatory Hill, British Consulate Hill, and the Inner Tidal Basin.

It may be arguable whether a regiment, already reduced by one battalion, should be landed in the very heart of a port installation. It will be remembered that at Dieppe, where the British commandos were entirely successful, the port was outflanked on each side before the main Canadian invasion force landed in the center, although with undeservedly catastrophic results. The failure was largely attributed to appalling security beforehand, so that the raid became common knowledge among the pubs in Portsmouth. The enemy was waiting. But prior bombardment on the Inchon scale would have overcome this disadvantage, just as it did at Inchon in the face of poor security. For *Operation Chromite* MacArthur was using men who, only ten days earlier, had been fighting in the Pusan perimeter. Not only could he afford fewer Marines, but it was essential to his strategy that the port and its facilities should be captured as soon as possible in order to allow the beachhead to be strengthened through the use of all the available harbor facilities. Both time and resources were at a premium, and because of these disadvantages he would continue to make every available use of the Navy and the Marine Air Wing. How would they tackle Red Beach?

Of prime importance to the planners of *Chromite* was the progress of the landing on Green Beach. That was the indicator of the enemy's ability to defend himself against such a surprise assault with massive naval and aerial bombardment. Not until noon, therefore, when success on Wolmi-do was assured, did the Americans begin to shell the main waterfront.

At that stage the transports and LST's for Red Beach were brought into the lee of the island, while another important preparation took place: The minesweepers arrived and cleared the channels. Capt. Lundgren of the *De Haven*, a former mine specialist, covered suspicious areas of water with 40 mm fire until he had reassured himself that no danger remained.

What the British would call a "warning order" was fully implemented at 1430 hours and Higgins' support ships began their final bombardment of Inchon by a deployment of those ships which had begun the task at noon. The four cruisers and six destroyers poured shells into the port for the next three hours, destroying every tactically important landmark and starting fires along the entire coastal strip, from Red to Blue. Supporting this, aircraft from Ewen's fast carriers defended the ships by sealing off the invasion area and using his heavy A.D.'s to hit targets and disrupt hostile movement within a 25-mile radius of Inchon. The USS *Boxer* arrived with more Corsairs and Ewen made ample use of them. From the VMF-214 and -323 came more Corsairs which were joined by three squadrons of the Navy's Skyraiders. These aircraft shared the hammering of Red Beach by careful stages from H-hour minus

180 minutes onward. Meanwhile, Task Force 77, by rotation, kept 12 aircraft aloft continuously to ensure that Inchon received no reinforcements from the interior. Closer inshore than the fast carriers, the *Sicily* and *Badoeng Strait*, which were normally jeep carriers, carried out an exacting flight schedule. The demand made on each pilot was considerable, for he was expected to perform two, and often three, missions in about only 20 hours. Particular mention should be made of the two most senior American pilots, Lt. Col. James N. Neefus and Lt. Col. Norman J. Anderson. On September 15th and 16th, the latter flew five sorties, which meant that he was airborne for 16 out of 24 hours. The concentration on Red Beach of countless 500- and 1,000-lb. bombs, 5-in. rockets and low-level strafing soon began to obscure the target area from both the sea and the sky, and heavy rain squalls mingled with the smoke and flames to create a bizarre sight. The butane tanks north of Red Beach burst into pale flame which turned slowly into jet smoke. "The whole area for miles around was obscured by smoke and debris and burning fires," [1] recalled Capt. Martin J. Sexton, Gen. Smith's aide.

It is impossible to apportion the responsibility for all this between the Navy and the Air Wing. At 1430 hours the naval impetus increased when the *Toledo* and *Rochester*, relying as before on air spotters, hit the eastern and northeastern sectors of Inchon with their 260-lb., 8-in. shells. While the *Jamaica* and *Kenya* were similarly bombarding Blue Beach, now with the assistance of spotters from the Fleet Air Arm's HMS *Triumph*, the 5th Marines' new task was being softened up by the 5-in. shells of the *De Haven* and *Swenson* which smashed every remaining military and industrial installation. By now, with the lower town burning fiercely, Doyle was confident that the assaults on Red and Blue Beaches could be launched simultaneously at 1730 hours.

What MacArthur had called "the second hand of destiny" [2] was now approaching that hour. At 1704 hours, in a heavy squall, the LCVP's carrying the leading companies were riding a mile offshore. From the air the craft could be seen to fan out before they raced for the shore, to disappear under a blanket of haze and smoke. But from the sea the marines, who only moments before had scrambled down the nets of the USS *Cavalier* and *Henrico*, were intent upon the flag of the Red Beach control vessel, *H.A. Bass*. The cruisers and destroyers were completing their missions when the invaluable rocket ship, LSMR-403, made her contribution to Red Beach. She proceeded to fling down 100 5-in. rockets a minute for the next 20 minutes on the beach and the northeastern end of the town. The red and white flag went up from the dip and, at 1724 hours, it went down with the effect of a starter's gun. The first eight LCVP's raced toward northern Inchon with their guns blazing. From left to right, boats 1 to 4 were parts of two assault platoons of A Company, 1st Battalion, who were to take Cemetery Hill and secure the left flank. In boats 5 to 8, Marines of E Company, 2nd Battalion, were to clear the right flank of the beach and seize British Consulate Hill. Meanwhile, the 3/5th Marines were supporting the assault with machine gun fire, mortars, and H.E. from M-26 Pershings. The causeway was at last cleared up to its eastern end by an engineer team under Tech. Sgt. Knox. This enabled the detachment of A Company's tanks to advance onto the mainland as soon as the initial assault waves had hit the beach. As before, the naval gunfire was halted at this stage and the torch handed on to the Corsairs. It was now that the first aerial casualty occurred among the allies when a Corsair, piloted by Col. Walter E. Lischeid, was shot down on the edge of Seoul. The air strikes had been so close to the advancing Marines that some LCVP's were even struck by empty shell cases from the 20-mm cannons of the AD's.

On the northern flank of the beachhead three of the four LCVP's struck the seawall and shuddered to a halt at 1733 hours, while boat 1, commanded by Tech. Sgt. Orvel F. Mc-Mullen and containing half his first platoon, was reduced by engine failure and bobbed up and down rather helplessly on the tide until it was eventually taken in tow. The rest of the first platoon, under Pl./Guide, Sgt. Charles D. Allen, scaled the wall from boat 2 in a manner reminiscent of infantrymen "going over the top"; indeed, not since 1918 had this stratagem been so evident, especially during the last two years of the Korean War. Enemy resistance from the north was surprisingly heavy, and several Marines were killed by a persistent light machine gun. Others in the extreme north were able only to advance a few yards inland. Further south the men had better luck. Boat 3, carrying 2nd Lt. Francis W. Muetzel and a squad of his Second Platoon, slipped through a breach in the seawall right under the muzzle of a machine gun which, although protruding safely from a pillbox, failed to fire. This is the kind of unforeseeable luck which, in toto, does much to determine the success or failure of every military adventure—in various degrees, according to the disparity of power which the two sides are prepared to mount. Boat 4 brought more Marines to join those safely ashore, but this time with the precious cargo of a 3.5-in. rocket launcher. The Corsairs were still putting down their curtain of cannon fire as the members of boat 4 flushed out Red Beach's first prisoners, six shaken and frightened young recruits of the NKPA.

Of advantage to the invaders was the direction of the wind which, blowing directly along the coast, carried the smoke screen between the defenders and the Marines, so that at water level the immediate front was as dense and lifeless as a sea fog on the Dogger Bank. One correspondent on the spot was Marguerite Higgins of *The Herald Tribune* who, her sex notwithstanding, landed with the 1st Battalion, 5th Marines (Lt. Col. Newton). Not since the Spanish Civil War had women, like Hemingway's third wife Martha Gellhorn, reported from under the muzzles of the rifles. Miss Higgins reported that Wolmi-do "looked as if a giant forest fire has just swept over it. . . ." [3] Her overall narrative was lurid:

> Beyond was Red Beach. As we strained to see it more clearly, a rocket hit a round oil tower and big, ugly smoke rings billowed up. The dockside buildings were brilliant with flames. Through the haze it looked as if the whole city was burning. . . . The strange sunset, combined with the brilliant haze of the flaming docks, was so peculiar that a movie audience would have considered it overdone.

The sight that presented itself to the men of the 1st and 2nd Battalions, 5th Marines, once they were over the wall, must have transported their minds to chaos. Beyond the beach on the left was Cemetery Hill, presenting an almost vertical bluff on its seaward side. The second wave was late on its target, and to avoid becoming trapped between the sea and any enemy who might suddenly appear at the foot of the bluff, Muetzel made straight for his objective, the Asahi Brewery, which, ignoring the flaming wreckage of the padlocked buildings, the Second Platoon reached unopposed after a march up an empty flamelicked street. But Muetzel could not hold it against strong resistance which suddenly poured from the east and his platoon had to change direction and assault the southeast of the hill. Newton had promised a pint of beer to each of his men if the brewery could be taken intact. But the prize would have to wait.

Meanwhile, the Marines over on the left were still being pinned down in the way that all amphibious mariners fear most, while the element of surprise that existed at first is slowly being eroded. The Third Platoon, under 1st Lt. Baldomero Lopez, landed in support of McMullen and the scaling ladders went up. Having shattered the first enemy bunker with a grenade, Lopez moved to the second and had removed the pin of a second grenade when he was hit under the right arm by a burst of machine gun fire. Without its pin the grenade fell to the ground and rolled away, almost beyond reach and within four seconds of explosion. "Grenade!" he yelled, and throwing himself forward he managed to cradle the explosion with his body as it blew up. The first Marine to be decorated at Inchon, he was posthumously awarded the Medal of Honor. Two more Marines attacked this bunker with flame throwers, but both were shot in the process. Still the communists were in control of this sector of the beach, although, in view of the NKPA withdrawal elsewhere, it was at best taking on the appearance of a holding action. The NKPA might suddenly realize the necessity of strengthening the investors of Pusan; or if despite that it seemed to them that retreat north would herald a rout, he would not present the U.N. with any more prisoners than necessary. Locally, at Inchon, the situation was eventually controlled with the landing at H + 5 minutes in Muetzel's sector by Capt. John R. Stevens' A Company which returned balance to the Marines upset by the loss of Lopez' leadership and the casualties among his men. Stevens had been unable to contact McMullen, but ordered his executive officer, 1st Lt. Fred F. Eubanks, Jr., to "take over on the left and get them organizing and moving." Time was now an essential factor since Cemetery Hill, the objective of the first platoon, still remained in enemy hands. But within the next half hour strong reinforcements would be landed at this point, although meanwhile Stevens contacted Muetzel and ordered his Second Platoon back to the beach to help out. On returning to the beach, Muetzel noticed an excellent route to the summit of Cemetery Hill, and in only 20 minutes, without a shot fired or a casualty sustained, Muetzel reached this important point and took several very dazed prisoners from the NKPA's 226th Regiment.

Eubanks succeeeded in overcoming the difficulties on the left before Muetzel returned, on the first occasion by a grenade duel and then immediately with flame throwers which the enemy could not match. The 1st and 3rd platoons now broke out of their restricted positions and made contact with Muetzel's men who were on their way to the beach, having captured Cemetery Hill. At 1775 hours Stevens confirmed that the hill had been secured by firing an amber star. The duel on the left flank of Red Beach had cost A Company eight killed and 28 wounded.

On the right, E Company had landed at 1731. The company commander, Capt. Samuel Jaskilka, ashore at H-hour plus ten minutes, ordered one of his platoons under 1st Lt. Edwin A. Deptula to make for the British Consulate Hill which enabled Observatory Hill itself to be covered, while Roise and the rest of the 2nd Battalion secured the base of the Wolmi-do causeway around the Nippon Flour Mill. Now all could turn their attention onto that formidable feature which loomed high above them.

But under more normal conditions, by assaulting an enemy who was not so unbalanced and had at least a modicum of strategic foresight (such as a tested and experienced European veteran of two world wars might expect), the Marines could have expected mounting difficulties at this stage. One of their pilots, Norman Anderson, flashed back the message to the

Mount McKinley from the smoke screened panorama over Red Beach, "Scaling ladders are in place and Marines are over the wall." Encouraging news though this was, it must be remembered that through the murk, dusk would soon descend over the scene, while the invaders were in fact still only perched on the beachhead, more evident now with the treacherously receding tide. Unlike Green Beach, the element of surprise had been lost at an early stage and the enemy, theoretically at least, could still observe from their big hill.

Then, in the fading light, came one of the most extraordinary sights and calculated risks of the whole operation. At 1800 hours eight LST's, formerly Japanese, very unmaneuverable fishing hulks now reinforced by steel on the fo'cstle and stem, waddled ashore towards Red Beach with a crew of inexperienced officers and men. The intention was to draw enemy fire and reveal the remaining disposition of the coastal defense batteries. While other LST's were still disgorging their precious cargo of heavy equipment, these eight craft were intended to distract the enemy. As they blazed their way ashore they placed a wide section of the beachhead in some jeopardy. The remaining NKPA obligingly let off everything they had at them, so being spotted in the process; but the LST's, maintaining the hoax, hit back, and Muetzel's platoon was blasted off the crest of Cemetery Hill toward Observatory Hill, which they preferred to the LST gunfire. One Marine was killed and 23 wounded in this extraordinary exercise. It smacked very much of MacArthurian unorthodoxy and one doubts its real validity. It may, however, have had the desired effect of distracting the defenders on the northern flank.

There had been a certain measure of the accustomed chaos of an amphibious landing, as evident in minor confusion and the flotsam of wooden packing cases and the arms-spread, face-down corpses, lapping with the soft plop of the water against the sea wall. Apart from the LCVP which had broken down, another commanded by Lt. Poul F. Pederson of C Company was pulled out of formation by the coxswain to assist the incapacitated vehicle, with the result that Pederson was dropped at the wrong place, at the wrong time, having narrowly missed being crushed by one of the trigger-happy, waddling LST's.

Two of Pederson's platoons, however, under 2nd Lts. Magness and Merritt, with the company's 60 mm mortars (and helped by the bravery of Tech. Sgt. Max Stein) managed to advance on to Observatory Hill, as planned. Magness signaled "objective taken," but his flare was a dud so that Newton failed to realize that there was a unit of his battalion above him on the hill. Accordingly, he ordered Capt. Fenton to achieve the object which he had detailed to Pederson. Fenton deployed one platoon to the left and advanced uphill with the other, meeting sporadic fire from the NKPA's 226th Regiment. He, too, reached the summit by 2000 hours and was surprised to find that C Company's second platoon was already there. But further confusion followed. 1st Lt. H. J. Smith, who commanded D Company on the 2nd Battalion's part of the hill, broke cover when "those treacherous old tubs," the LST's, had stopped firing and he then made for the top of the hill, via the railway yard. Believing that E Company was already installed on the hill, Smith advanced confidently up the main road to save time, encountering near the top not Marines, but North Koreans who immediately opened fire. The Americans hit the deck and took what cover they could find on the scorched and warm hillside which burned here and there like myriad fireflies. They were mighty relieved to be supported, after a short time, by the more cautious men of D Company.

The most fundamental cause of the chaos was under rehearsal. It was no fault of the commander of the control vessel *H.A. Bass*, Lt. Cmdr. Ralph H. Schreenloch, who was using proper control procedure and radio contact with the forward elements on the beach, that the second wave did not approach the shore in the correct manner; indeed, there was a mixing of waves, starting with LSVP number 4. The result was that parts of C and D companies, both in the second assault, landed on the wrong beaches. The mistake was only compounded by Pederson's misfortune or misjudgment. It is easier with hindsight to criticize momentary decisions, but Pederson would have been better advised to ignore his unfortunate comrades in the drifting LCVP and make straight for his allotted landing zone. The area of slight overlap, where the two battalions' flanks joined one another, had become congested and confused, and with the heavy smoke and failing light the Marines had temporary difficulty in finding their own platoons. They were lucky to get away so lightly; without the bombardment the enemy would have wreaked havoc with an amphibious error like that, but then without the bombardment, Inchon would never have succeeded as it did.

But the fighting, vitiated more by confusion than actual loss of life (which was still remarkably light, despite the trouble in the north of the beachhead), was yet not as tough as had been foreseen. On the right of the 5th Marines gains were more swiftly made, despite the handicaps of confused double boat waves, the LST fire, and poor visibility. There were no casualties in following the arc down to the British Consulate Hill, except in boat 3. The worst confusion in this sector was that already mentioned on the southern flank of Observatory Hill. The only objective still left in enemy hands along the line of the 3,000-yard front was the tidal basin.

Night had now fallen and it was pitch dark. Roise was reluctant to send more Marines into Inchon until dawn. He consulted Murray who had come ashore at 1830 hours and set up his command post near the mainland end of the causeway, and was told by Gen. Smith that where the O-A Line could not actually be defended from a suitable tactical position it must at least be covered by a reconnaissance patrol which could report back if there were any movement in the area. Roise immediately sent a patrol from F Company to the tidal basin, and his small force returned from an 1,100-yard recce into Inchon at 2300 hours. Consequently Roise placed F Company, less this platoon, from Observatory Hill along a defensive perimeter on the right flank. Just after midnight Capt. Vel E. Peters deployed his company next to the tidal basin, and the O-A Line, although not entirely manned, was as complete as the tangled conurbation in dark conditions would allow. All was quiet along the front and, with the exception of the basin (which was carefully outposted), Red Beach had been completely captured by midnight. Otherwise, only one mission had not yet been achieved—there was no beer for Newton's thirsty Marines.

CHAPTER FIVE

Blue Beach:
The Chaos of Symmetry

Now the upper cut! In strictly pugilistic terms this would have been difficult because it occurred at precisely the same moment as the left hook, but geographically it illustrates the situation. Nearly four miles down the coast from the main targets was the relatively lone (but no less important) assault, south of Inchon, which MacArthur's planners called *Blue Beach*. It was to prove essential in helping to ensnare the enemy between the anvil of Inchon and the hammer of the Eighth Army which was still holding its ground under General Walker's command in the Pusan perimeter. From the conquerors of Blue Beach would fan out those Marines, together with the 7th Infantry Division, who were to link up with Walker's long trek northward. But Blue Beach was also important in the context of the strategy of Inchon itself; particularly when the three-pronged force eventually drove its Marines onto nearly every side of Seoul. But, in any case, the shape of the coastline adjacent to Inchon demanded that two separate and simultaneous assaults should be made, since the coast south of the port was a wide sweeping inlet which had to be held down to its southern extremity, Tok Am.

Here was the most complicated task facing the invaders and one which, despite the utmost gallantry by those Marines concerned, proved to be the most chaotic. Chaos, as every veteran knows, is experienced almost as much by the victors as by the vanquished. The ear-splitting din makes it seem that only a very rough approximation to the plan is being executed. The landing on Blue Beach was complicated because the invaders

86

A Navy Corsair *patrolling above United Nations War and Supply ships near the Inchon beachhead.* (Photo courtesy of U.S. Navy Department.)

LCM's (Landing Craft, Mechanized) racing against a strong tide towards Blue Beach. (Photo courtesy of U.S. Army.)

Aerial view showing the typical use of LCVP's (Landing Craft, Vehicle and Personnel) in an amphibious assault in Korea, a month after Inchon. (Photo courtesy of U.S. Navy Department.)

LCVP's and LST's (Landing Ship, Tank) waiting their turn to go up to the pontoon docks to unload replacements of U.S. Marine troops and supplies. (Photo courtesy of U.S. Navy Department.)

MacArthur, surrounded by his staff, acknowledges the victory of his Marines on Green Beach. (Photo courtesy of U.S. Navy Department.)

LST's unloading their supplies on Red Beach, September 15, 1950. (Photo courtesy of U.S. Navy Department.)

Sgt. W. W. Frank at the head of his platoon on one of the scaling ladders on Red Beach. (Photo courtesy of U.S. Defense Department.)

A photograph taken exactly seven years after the Inchon landing, showing the statue of General Douglas MacArthur after its unveiling at Inchon. (Photo courtesy of U.S. Army.)

Douglas MacArthur, after handing over control to Syngman Rhee, aggressively anticipates the next stage of his campaign. (Photo courtesy of Robert Hunt Library.)

had to deliver two widely separated amphibious assaults in order to tie up the entire coastline of the bight, and spread thence to occupy a wide stretch of country inland, northward between Inchon and Seoul and southward to link up with the Eighth Army, in the unlikely event of misfortune to the 7th Infantry Division. Between Marines and soldiers there was always an undercurrent of acrimony.

All the more surprising, therefore, was the fact that the 1st Marines were used here, because, despite an honorable history in the Second World War, they had already been disbanded, taking with them the memory of the great actions at the Boxer Risings, Veracruz, Nicaragua, Guadalcanal, New Britain, Peleliu, and Okinawa. But now to their rescue came Col. Puller, the bluff old warrior who had much in common with his chief. His mission was to land south of Inchon and seize the main approach to the port from the south, then advance directly on Yongdungpo, the capital's main suburb, and so to Seoul. For this task he was given two beaches; the 2nd Battalion (Lt. Col. Allan Sutter) on the left and the 3rd Bn. (Lt. Col. Thomas L. Ridge) on the right. The reserve consisted of the 1st Battalion (Lt. Col. Jack Hawkins) who would follow Ridge over Blue Beach 2. A further breakdown of this deployment was as follows:

2nd Battalion (Blue One)
(Sutter)

ABLE: This was the code name of a critical road junction, just over a thousand yards northeast of the beach which had to be seized.

DOG: This referred to Hill 117,* 3,000 yards northeast of the beach, commanding Inchon's back door and the road leading to Seoul, 22 miles away. This, likewise, had to be taken urgently.

3rd Battalion (Blue Two)
(Ridge)

CHARLIE: A seaward tip of Hill 233, a long east-west ridge beginning 1,500 yards southeast of the beach and sealing off the

* Hill numbers in Korea, of course, always referred to the height of the features in meters.

stubby Munhang Peninsula which projects southward. Vitally important.

BAKER: A small cape, topped by Hill 94, to the right of objective *Charlie* and flanking Blue Beach.

Blue Beach had both advantages and disadvantages. Chief among the latter, of course, was the beach's width. Here alone the invaders, requiring speed to cover the initial beachhead against the advancing dusk, used amtracs (amphibious tractors). But Blue Beach was poor for amphibious operations because it required a two-and-a-half-mile approach over mudflats which involved a 45-minute run in to land the Marines. The nature of the landing zone was particularly uninviting because Blue Beach was overlooked by an abrupt hillock only a few yards inland. On the right side of the hill a fetid ditch found a wide and muddy effluence and divided the beaches. Blue's first ingress was a dirt road, winding around the hill's left shoulder, and when Ridge approached it he could see at once that the width of the cove might render the beach useless.

But, on the other hand, Blue Beach did enjoy one evident advantage, denied to the other two beaches: The Marines here had greater elbow room, more beach (however awkward), and less constricting urban space in which to fight. But to take advantage of this wide front it was essential to bombard simultaneously both jaws of the beach, particularly the sharp southern promontory, Tok Am. Here the British cruisers particularly showed their worth, and HMS *Jamaica* struck an ammunition dump with her 6-in. shells which caused an explosion that rocked the Orient.

Each of the Blue Beaches was 500 yards wide; and Blue Beach 2, like the Red Beaches, was fronted by a rock seawall which would have to be scaled by ladders from the LVT's; while around the corner, on the right of this beach, was a small cove, subsequently found, called Blue Beach 3, which was considered as a possible secondary landing site. But here, as before, we must now examine the nature of the bombardment and the ship-to-shore movement which turned out to be even more disastrous than that which rushed towards Red Beach. It duly came under stern rebuke from Col. Puller, a man admired from a distance but regarded by his immediate subordinates as a military martinet. But he was an experienced Marine who realized only too well that speed on his beach was of prime importance because "Once on the O-1 Line, the 1st Marines would flank the single overland approach to the peninsula seaport, thereby presenting the NKPA garrison with the grim alternative of early flight, capitulation or strangulation. Without this leverage on Inchon's flank and rear, the 5th Regiment could easily be swallowed up by two square miles of dense urban area." [1] It now remained to be seen, as the 1st and 5th Marines' forward units reached Inchon, whether the four assault battalions could achieve this interdependent venture before nightfall, two hours later.

Only the cruisers, *Jamaica* and *Kenya*, then, added to the pre-D-Day heavy bombardment of Blue Beach. There were no American cruisers here. But while the *Jamaica* continued to pound the high ground behind the beach the USS *Gurke* and *Henderson* struck at the rear and flanks of the target area with their 5-in. shells. Now, as before, came the rocket ships LSMR-401 and -402, well in shore on each side of the boating lanes, to fire 2,000 5-in. rockets onto the spits and jaws of the bight. The USS *Gurke*, which had already been hit several times by shore batteries and was the most unfortunate of the allied warships, and the USS *Wantuck* both came under heavy fire which they returned.

At 1400 hours the Blue Beach landing force commander saw the first landing craft anticipate the heavy naval traffic by moving towards their respective command boats. The Blue Beach control vessel, the destroyer USS *Diachenko*, now moved to her station 3,000 yards southwest of the Blue Beach line of departure. Her captain, Lt. Cmdr. Allman, checked the drift of the current which was so important to establish with a long approach, to ensure that the boats landed at their correct destinations. He radioed his findings to Adm. Doyle, and both sailors were surprised that the estimated current was as swift as 3½ knots; but nevertheless Doyle confirmed that 1730 hours was satisfactory for H-Hour. At H-25 minutes Adm. Higgins signalled for both cruisers and destroyers to cease fire and for the LSMR's to take over. At 1645 hours 18 Army LVT(A)'s, with the first wave of the 1st Marines, crossed the line and set off over the 5,500 yards to the beach which would not be reached for three-quarters of an hour, while the vehicles crawled in at four knots enfiladed by the current.

Meanwhile, there had been some anxiety over the amtracs. As H-Hour approached the NKPA, with full intelligence of the Marines' intentions, turned what vengeance they had to spare onto the newly launched little vehicles, but Doyle refused permission for a temporary withdrawal while the naval force resumed its softening up for a little longer. Thus ordered, 172 of them began racing toward the beach. But at this point another difficulty arose, and the U.S.N. Beach Control Officer noted that only four of the Navy's guide boats were available to shepherd in 25 boat waves, whereas he reckoned that at least 32 should have been earmarked for such a mission. There begins to emerge an extraordinary disparity of resources for *Operation Chromite*. While there seemed to be nothing spared to support the invasion, men and invasion craft were less easily obtainable than the heavy weapons. Remembering Adm. Andrewes' remark, it seems that Gen. MacArthur considered that only by swamping the North Koreans with sheer weight of weapons could he succeed where the Pentagon's frugality in other directions would have completely precluded the success of *Operation Chromite*. Such resistance as there was and evidence of bunkers and emplacements, makes one wonder whether the enemy's rear, especially in the immediate area of Seoul, was as ill-defended as MacArthur contended.

The LSMR's had continued to pump their rockets in high-arched trajectory onto Blue Beach, right up to the moment when the LVT's were within 2,000 yards of the beach, and when the amtracs landed, the Corsairs, in customary fashion, cleared a zone 50 yards ahead of the Marines. But for all supporting arms the task was becoming increasingly difficult, owing to the pall of smoke. Whereas earlier that day the wind down-coast had effectively helped what was still an element of surprise (this now having been lost and with Inchon's industrial installations burning more fiercely than ever), the beach precisely downwind was made invisible to the landing force by a sulphurous haze, and it isolated the precise naval targets from the LSMR's as it had done from the bigger ships. But whenever the U.S. Marines are given a difficult assignment, albeit not these days on the scale of Inchon, the Navy is the first to experience the handicaps. A typical problem confronting naval planners was cited by Major Edwin H. Simmons of the 3rd Battalion, 1st Marines:

> I was aboard LST-802, which was carrying H and S Companies and elements of Weapons Company. The ship had just been recovered from the island trade. Her captain had been flown out to Sasebo from the States, given a pick-up crew and two weeks to condition the ship and crew for an amphibious landing. Despite his best efforts, the -802 had three major breakdowns and had to drop out of the convoy several times. At one point it appeared as though the Batallion Command Group would have to be taken off the -802 if they were to get to Inchon at all.[2]

In connection with Blue Beach itself, officers of the 1st Marines had only a vague impression of offshore conditions and the accessibility of the landing site. The channel current, as I have noted, had been underestimated, and so little was known about the consistency of the mudflats that each craft contained planking in case of emergency. I have referred to the misgiving of Puller's men when they saw the wide extent of the mudflats. Instead of a relatively clear shoreline the men saw a murky wall rolling seaward from the blazing waterfront. The current caused considerable difficulty to the proper formation of the vessels in the RV area, and another obstacle was described by Lt. Clark, the Blue Beach Control Officer:

> At about H-50, while press boats and the initial wave of LVT(A)'s and LVT's were milling around Blue Beach control vessel (Wantock), mortar fire was received in the immediate vicinity. This created some confusion until a destroyer spun around on her anchor and silenced the battery. This was the beginning of the end of the well planned ship-to-shore movement for Blue Beach.[3]

The U.S. Navy had over-reacted.

The 1st Marines, which like the rest was supported by every

weapon in the American arsenal, was nevertheless poorly equipped with much that was vital to any amphibious operation, a shortage to which Marines pointed as evidence of the shabby way the Corps had become treated by the Pentagon under the stewardship of Louis Johnson and Gen. Bradley. Puller complained bitterly that "the naval control of the ship-to-shore movement was very poor and almost nonexistent." [4] But the weather and man-made obstructions were the chief culprits, although the absence of equipment to deal with these was summed up by another report from Major Simmons:

> We had been told that a wave guide would pick us up and lead us to the line of departure. . . . Two LCVP's did come alongside our wave. The first was filled with photographers. The second was loaded with Korean interpreters. Two of these were hastily dumped into my LVT, apparently under the mistaken notion that I was a battalion commander. Both interpreters spoke Korean and Japanese; neither spoke English. Time was passing and we were feeling faintly desperate when we came alongside what apparently was the central control vessel. I asked the bridge for instructions. A naval officer with a bullhorn pointed out the direction of Blue Two, but nothing could be seen in that direction except smoke. We were on our way, and our path crossed that of another wave. I asked if they were headed for Blue Two. Their wave commander assured, "Hell, no. We're the 2nd Battalion headed for Blue One." We then veered off to the right. I broke out my map and asked the LVT driver if he had a compass. He looked at his instrument panel and said, "Search me, six weeks ago I was driving a truck in San Francisco." [5]

It is almost unbelievable. Was there no quartermaster? But in fairness to the U.S. Marine Corps, it must be said that the unique and natural difficulties at Inchon meant that all the old and well-tried naval/marine principles evolved in the Pacific war had to be discarded.

The first three waves reached their allotted positions on time, Puller successfully landing with the third; but confusion increased as the guide boats, at the whim of the wind, were unable to see their targets. Puller's men had certainly collected all the day's pollution from three beaches, carried by a wind which synchronized its switch towards the southwest with the invasion's thrust towards the east. Not all, however, were unfortunate; and waves which landed as planned contained the officers and men needed for a successful perch, at least, along the wide front. On Blue Beach 1, Sutter's D and F assault companies landed without opposition. The exit road to the left was blocked by a slide owing to air strikes and naval gunfire, so the advance inland was impassable for D Company. F, however, soon scaled a hill overlooking Blue 1 and with 600 more men ashore Sutter deployed them as swiftly as possible, while considering anxiously the fate of the rest of the 2nd Battalion whose amtracs had gone astray.

To the right, on Blue 2, Army amphibious tanks still lay offshore, firing at specific enemy targets which were trying to prevent a substantial American build-up at this point. These were overtaken by the leading wave of amtracs towards the ditch, up which G Company advanced before scaling the ladders. Only moderate enemy fire was encountered here. Meanwhile, like Sutter, Ridge (3 Bn.) had made an early landing. A member of his battalion, a certain Maj. Reginald R. Myers, soon realized that a third Blue Beach, already mentioned, could be opened beyond a cove on his right flank. Tractors were duly landed and beached at right angles to Blue 2. Now nearly all the other amtracs began to arrive on Myers' impromptu beachhead, Blue 3. Thus at 1800 hours (at the same moment when, further up the coast, the eight LST's were rushing at Red Beach), despite appalling weather which seemed to be deteriorating, all the battalions had their respective assault companies ashore, and Ridge and Sutter were taking charge. When Puller brought in his own amtracs in the third wave the landing was almost complete.

We have already seen how each feature was to be taken and we know something of the broad responsibility of the Battalion commanders of Puller's 1st Marines. There was some conveniently hollow ground leading from the center of the southeast of Blue Beach which was occupied by Ridge's G Company. But Sutter was less fortunate. With only part of his battalion ashore he ordered D and F Companies (all he then possessed) to advance to their respective objectives, the road junction and an area half a mile inland on the left flank; and Hill 117 from which the best view would be had of the land leading eastwards towards Yongdungpo and the Han River where X Corps had to expect fierce resistance. D Company duly captured the road junction as dusk was approaching and by 2200 hours F Company was well entrenched on Hill 117, ready to block the road. Considering his shortage Sutter had done well; and considering, too, that throughout the whole operation he was consistently to be the most unfortunate battalion commander, his skill and resolve were to continue to be evident. But in human terms, soon after his landing, he claimed 15 communist prisoners and the lives of 50 of their comrades, while his battalion sustained only one fatal and 19 wounded casualties.

Over on the right the 3rd Battalion had broken out of the ditch under the firm leadership of one of Ridge's ablest officers, Capt. J. G. Westover.* Immediately, Lt. James R. Fisher made off southward to try to take the western spur of Hill 233 before dusk concealed this greatest threat to Blue Beach. The gap between Westover's and Fisher's men was covered by the reserve company which had landed on Myers' Blue Beach 3. It was clear from the overall deployment of his men that Puller was trying to move the Marines of Blue Beach southward as fast as possible in order to widen the overall beachhead and secure it at the most convenient southern spot, and occupy the forward slopes of the high ground while light still permitted. He confidently reported to Gen. Smith at 0130 hours, D+1, that the beach was taken, and before bedding down in a gulley under a poncho he handed a folded set of colors to his radioman with the remark, "You keep this . . . we're going to fly it over Seoul." [6]

The chief problem now, the occupation of the initial beachhead line notwithstanding, was to get the remaining guide boats ashore. Smoke still obscured everything. Those Marines destined for Blue 2 (for we are still considering the dusk movements, before Puller's message) found themselves on Blue 1.

* See General Military Bibliography.

Chaos, indeed! A searchlight of an LVT was turned on to the beach, but its glare was misdirected northward, which only made matters worse. Thus Hawkins, Puller's reserve commander, landed over two miles to the left of the beaches, on the outer seawall of Inchon's tidal basin which, of course, was the only feature not yet controlled by Murray's 5th Marines. Hawkins immediately understood the situation (which would probably not have occurred had the forces been properly equipped) and set off southward in angry and defiant mood toward Blue Beach which, with a large catch of prisoners and a hearty welcome from C Company, 2nd Battalion, 1st Marines, they reached early next morning. The sun had gone down on September 15th on another naval-shore engagement when the *Gurke* (hit yet again) and the LSMR-401, also damaged, together managed to silence those shore batteries which had miraculously survived the heaviest localized scorch-up in modern times.

Chaotic though the closing stages of the day continued to be, the force was essentially ashore and the commanders back on the *Mount McKinley* had cause for joy and relief, particularly since no semblance of a rehearsal had been held. For some young draft Marines Inchon was the first occasion on which they had ever made an amphibious landing and, Iwon apart, it would be the last.

Now came the follow-up—the landing and registration of armor and heavy vehicles over all beaches—an operation amid the glare of lights from every direction which drew the enemy's enfilade fire as a candle draws a moth. This would continue until D+2. One former gunnery sergeant, later Lt. Col. Jim Crowe, proved his outstanding leadership and organizing ability in this complicated logistical operation. Bulldozers with blades came ashore and, like elephants hauling teak logs, they pushed the harbor wall into the sea in several awkward places to allow the landing of 450 vehicles aboard the LST's. While this matter of fact business was taking place along the waterfront on D+2 local authority was being handed back by MacArthur personally to the South Koreans in the person of the former deputy mayor of Inchon.

By the close of D-Day, Admiral Doyle had put 13,000 Marines ashore* on a terrible coastline together with all their weapons and equipment and much heavy armor. Despite certain determined pockets of resistance, such as that on the northern front of Red Beach, the losses had been even lighter than expected. Twenty-one U.S. servicemen had been killed, one was missing and 174 had been wounded. Of the NKPA's casualties there is no record. The civilian deaths must have been astronomic. As in all modern wars this complicates the priorities between morality (if that is a sufficient word) and military expediency. But, speaking strictly from a military point of view, Gen. Smith said that D-Day had "gone about as planned."

* Starting at 0630 hours, the Americans put 23,000 men ashore on Utah Beach on D-Day, 1944.

CHAPTER SIX

The Battle for Kimpo Airfield

The beachheads were virtually secured, but obscure problems lay ahead. The victors of Red and Blue Beaches, now incorporating the Battalion under Lt. Col. Taplett which had swept through Wolmi-do, had to race to the next line, called O-3, in preparation for their anticipated hard slog against Kimpo Airfield, Yongdungpo, the crossing of the Han River, and the capture of Seoul where strong resistance was expected, while vigilantly taking every opportunity to facilitate the break out of Gen. Walker's Eighth Army. Puller's regiment, then, had to spread itself widely across the interior and south of its landing zone. Now that the element of surprise was gone, speed was necessary, and it was essential for the Marines to watch out for any communist build-up until the arrival of the 7th Division, U.S. Army, under Maj. Gen. David G. Barr to support the weary invaders.

Now the U.S. Marine Air Wing could take a look at the interior, beyond the furthest reaches of the Marines' advance, and early on D+1 Corsairs from the flight deck of USS *Sicily* were aloft, over the beachhead and making for the route from Seoul to reconnoiter the disposition of the enemy's armor which, quite correctly, they felt would be advancing down the road from the capital towards Inchon. This was the period when, until the arrival of the Army to strengthen their numbers, the Marines needed aerial support, and none looked forward more eagerly to the sortie as these aircraft as they disappeared toward the rising sun. Crossing the next line of assault, the O-3, and following the road and railway—always a pilot's navigational

97

delight—they soon spotted their quarry. Near some huts marked on the map as Kansong-ni, six T-34 tanks were churning a dirt track towards Sutter's 2nd Battalion on Blue Beach. Maj. Floeck and his men rolled their Corsairs over in turn and descended towards the vehicles, hitting them with napalm and rocket salvos. This checked the advance of three of them, enveloping two in orange flame, but with the loss of one aircraft piloted by Capt. Simpson whose Corsair was hit in the air cooler by an anti-aircraft tracer shell of the keenly accurate NKPA anti-aircraft defenses. A second sortie at 0650 hours knocked out two more tanks and strafed a large number of infantry who had no cover in sight. Some clue had now been obtained of the communists' strength and awareness, as yet relatively slight, and D+1 had started with the same spirit of urgency as its predecessor.

But the force beachhead had yet to be won beyond all doubt, so that Gen. Smith could come ashore to resume command of the 1st Marine Division. The omens were promising so far as the latest battle was concerned, for the NKPA had sustained unexpectedly heavy losses in armor, in addition to the tanks destroyed by the Corsairs, and it was clear that the enemy was anxious, as far as possible, to make this a tank war in such evidently suitable country, as the Germans, and then the Russians, had done over Germany's eastern front in World War II.

The second night at Inchon was quiet, and at first light the reserve South Korean Marines, under a resolute if undiscriminating officer called Lt. Col. Shin Hyun-jun, gave the place a "mopping up," an operation left to those who had better knowledge of the country. The communists had wrought such carnage in their advance southward in June that non-sympathizers, such as these Marines, did not question too closely those whom they suspected of having collaborated with the enemy, and the Americans tended to turn a blind eye to this stage of the operations which revolted those Europeans who had been able to acquit their sense of duty more easily by decimating the place from a distance of two miles.

The first task of Col. Murray's 5th Marines on Red Beach was to link up with Puller and his men further south and close the gap in the beachhead. Thus Roise's 2nd Battalion, 5th Marines, joined Sutter's 2nd Battalion, 1st Marines, on Hill 117.

But Puller, as I have emphasized, had a harder task because he had to ensure the safety of his own beach on its southern flank. In order to do this he sent Lt. Col. Ridge with his 3rd Battalion southward to the Munhang Peninsula to seek out any remaining NKPA's. Advancing from Hill 233 Ridge moved down easily, curved around the rugged cape, and returned to Blue Beach. The expedition had been rewarding, for he brought back a substantial number of prisoners and discovered a deserted coastal defense battery and a haul of arms, including a large quantity of vicious Russian-made 120 mm mortars of ill-repute in Korea.

In the north of his beachhead Puller ensured that his 2nd Battalion kept in close touch with the 5th Marines as they jointly advanced inland towards what had become known as "Ascom City" which had once been a U.S. forces' supply depot, now given its sobriquet from the words "Army Service Command," and which represented the pivot of the main line of consolidation behind the beachhead. This was particularly the responsibility of Col. Bowser, a Marine staff officer who had been a dedicated protagonist of the Inchon campaign from the beginning. He had planned both the advance on Ascom City and the approach by the 2nd Battalion, 5th Marines, towards Kansong-ni which the Corsairs had reconnoitered the previous day. This seems to have been an area favored by the enemy for tank reconnaissance and patrol because now, for the first time, a tank duel took place between a section of Pershings, under 2nd Lt. Joseph Sleger, covering a steep hill (186) east of the road, and three T-34's on the road below them. The old Russian warhorses were supplied only with manually powered hand-crank turrets which were too slow for the hydraulically driven turrets of the Pershings which, before the T-34's could even take aim, had fired off 20 90 mm armor-piercing shells which burned out the enemy vehicles in seconds. The NKPA's T-34's were vanishing fast.

Murray was ordered to continue the advance, so he placed Taplett's reserve battalion at Wolmi-do in the line on Roise's left, and both battalions confidently moved out into the sparsely populated country at 1330 hours on D+1; in fact, no enemy was sighted, except a few snipers who were flushed out in the economical way made peculiar to American Marines by their technico-military efficiency. The operation was short and some

NKPA's were stripped naked for thorough examination. The position by 1600 hours was that Taplett's 3rd Battalion had reached their objective, having taken 12 prisoners and sustained no losses, while Roise had placed a company on each side of the hills covering the road and railway defiles before dusk.

Puller's wider front did not reach the O-3 Line until 1600 hours, for Sutter's least fortunate 2nd Battalion had met resistance in ground suitable for defense, where the road and railway pass through defiles over which the defenders had a better view of Inchon and Kansong-ni; indeed, the terrain south and west of Ascom City was well supplied with natural defensive positions. Nevertheless, the defense was quickly broken, but it is significant to note that all four fatal casualties came from Sutter's battalion, as did ten of the Division's 21 wounded men.

By dusk on D+1 it could be claimed that Gen. Smith's beachhead line was virtually secured, although no unit was actually on the position which had been so ambitiously placed well inland from Inchon. But the 5th Marines held high ground overlooking Ascom City and commanded the forward beachhead line. Puller's 1st Marines, however, were still a mile away, although his 1st and 2nd Battalions held key features. The situation which was worrying Puller most was his insecure southern flank. While Ridge moved from the Munhang reconnaissance area to reserve positions, Capt. Kenneth Houghton's Divisional Reconnaissance Company, which had landed in the afternoon from Green Beach after a wearying time in their pitching boats before the control vessel would allow them to come ashore, moved to the flank guard. Houghton's instructions were to cover the 1st Regiment's far right flank and, next day, to sweep the Namdong Peninsula, east of Munhang. This was a revealing exercise. On his sector of Puller's front Houghton found a large quantity of box mines, 40 tons of flaked TNT and nearly 2,000 cases of other explosives of American origin, captured from the South Korean forces in June. Meanwhile, Taplett, on the left of the 5th Marines, found a large vehicle park west of Ascom City, and another dump stocked high with U.S. ammunition.

But now everyone in high command was eager to get ashore. In the afternoon Shepherd and Almond, accompanied by a staff officer, Col. Krulak, and other aides, landed on Yellow Beach which, centrally placed, had just been opened in the inner har-

bor. First, they inspected Red Beach and Wolmi-do and visited
the wounded on a hospital LST. When Almond returned to the
Mount McKinley for lunch Shepherd borrowed Brig. Gen.
Craig's jeep and searched for Puller, and in the late afternoon
Adm. Struble came ashore to inspect the beaches, no doubt to
see for himself how accurate Higgins' gunnery had been.

The command structure now assumed a more formalized
appearance. Craig, an early and keen advocate of the Inchon
landings and a former commander of the 1st Marine Brigade,
was Smith's Chief of Staff, and with another staff officer,
Col. Stewart, he established Gen. Smith's headquarters on Yellow Beach and there raised the flag. Accordingly, Smith resumed command ashore and on taking leave of his Commander
in Chief he was told encouragingly, "Be sure to take care of
yourself, and capture Kimpo as soon as you can." Smith was
welcomed ashore by Craig and Stewart, and was surprised to
see that the Fleet Commander from the *Rochester* had preceded him. Making a swift reconnaissance of the beachhead,
Smith went first to visit Puller and was encouraged by the sight
of a large catch of prisoners on Sutter's sector.

It was now D+2. During the preceding night, September
16–17th, the enemy had implemented its first hurried plans to
discover the strength and position of the Americans' most forward thrust. The unit selected for this task, as the invaders
would discover, was the 2nd Battalion of the 1st Seoul Defense
Division and a tank platoon of the 42nd Mechanized Regiment.
The nature of the country eastward of the coastal ridges determined the lines on which heavy vehicles could move. This had
soon been established by the Marines' first aerial sorties. The
deployment of outposts, therefore, was a relatively simple business; and it was obvious to any commander that these inland
ridges had to be occupied first to give the Marines a clear view
of the NKPA's approach. The communists duly advanced along
the road from Yongdungpo to Ascom City, unwittingly approaching country which was either occupied by or under the
gaze of Sutter's battalion on the northern sector of Puller's 1st
Marines. We now know that the NKPA commander planned to
push his left-hand company across the ridges, including the important Hill 186 to his front, towards Kansong-ni. His right-
hand company of tanks would, meanwhile, have easier going

down the road, through Ascom City, and straight to the coast above Inchon. It was the infantry's task to secure this approach by gaining and holding the ridges beyond Ascom.

So much for the enemy. Not knowing his plans precisely, it was the task of D Company, 5th Marines, to halt Kim Il-sung on this front and destroy his forces, which they achieved with admirable, if ruthless, swiftness. The company halted on a hill with a road on its right and the Seoul–Inchon railway on its left, at the point where, about 350 yards to the northeast, the road turns suddenly eastwards (to the right) on its entry into Ascom City. Overlooking this road, forward of D Company's position, was another hill which Murray immediately recognized as being of strategic importance to the Marines. The most forward platoon commander, Lt. H. J. Smith, ordered his Second Platoon Leader, 2nd Lt. Lee R. Howard, a machine gun section and a 2.36-in. bazooka man, to dig into a position from which it could command the road.

Back towards Kanson-ni, in the defile between D and F Companies, Colonel Murray had posted the Regiment's 75 mm recoilless rifles (known to the men as "75 reckless") near the 3.5-in. rocket launchers of Roise's 2nd Battalion, 5th Marines. Further back, but closely coordinated with this deployment, were all five Pershings of the Tank Battalion's First Platoon, A Company. A well-coordinated pocket of firepower was now laid, and all the Americans had to do was to sit and wait.

Sure enough, through the patches of early morning ground fog, came the unmistakable whine, clank, and growl of T-34 tanks which soon showed themselves to be clad with hitching infantry (hardly good fieldcraft for a patrol in unknown country), while other foot soldiers advanced astride the vehicles. The sight was more like a casual crowd going to a football match and was hardly suitable formation to adopt when approaching rising ground from which an enemy could have a clear field of fire. But the safety of lives has never been a prime consideration of communist armies. In all, six tanks appeared through the mist, accompanied by evidently ill-trained infantry. From their positions commanding a view straight down the road on a perfectly sited ridge, Howard and his men held their fire while the high-spirited force of NKPA sauntered leisurely towards its imminent doom. Then, when the enemy was fully within the pocket, the Marines let rip from every side. The enemy infantry tumbled off their tanks, either to rush for sparse cover or fall dead. Some limped off and others fell under the tanks' tracks. The bazookaman, Cpl. C. J. Douglas, ran to within 75 yards of one T-34 and slammed in a 2.36-in. rocket, causing the vehicle virtually to disintegrate in the accustomed orange flame. Then the Pershings opened up with 45 high velocity 90 mm shells which had the most devastating effect. The recoilless rifles from both Roise's and Sutter's battalions found their marks, followed by the scorching from Roise's 3.5-in. rocket launchers, recently used widely by the I.R.A. in Ulster, which were then the infantryman's latest weapon. It was by way of an encore that Marine Walter Monegan made special use of his launcher by tackling the only serviceable tank still remaining at point-blank range and proving the undoubted adequacy of this new device.

Then there was a long strange silence. The whining tanks lay in smashed heaps, and the infantrymen either lay still or crawled with irremediable wounds across the dew-damp earth. All six tanks had been knocked out and at least 200 men lay dead on the road and its verges. It was a sight which even the most vehement anti-communist could hardly relish.

Now, after an early breakfast on this bloody morning, Gen. MacArthur, with Adm. Struble and Gens. Shepherd, Almond, Ruffner (deputy commander of X Corps), Hodes (Almond's Chief of Staff), Fox, Whitney (both senior staff officers), and Wright (MacArthur's G3 and Deputy Chief of his Planning Staff), with an army of reporters which included Marguerite Higgins, were greeted at Yellow Beach by Gen. Smith. First, MacArthur wanted to call on Puller (which seemed to have been an habitual priority among visiting generals), whose southern flank was the most vulnerable. The colonel, atop Hill 186, had no time to go down to greet the Commander in Chief and is reported to have said, "If he wants to see me, have him come up in the front lines. I'll be waiting for him." [1] Eagerly the General puffed his way up the hill, showing remarkable vigor for a man of over 70, while Puller was planning his move forward to the next ridge, Hill 132. "We thought we'd find you back in the C.P. (command post)," said an officer. "That's my C.P.!," [2] said Puller, slapping the high ground on his map with the back of his hand. Then MacArther interjected, "Colonel, your regiment is performing splendidly, and I am grateful to present you with the Silver Star." Unfortunately, the General's A.D.C. had failed to bring any decorations from the *Mount McKinley.* "Then make a note of that," said MacArthur. He also instructed that Col. Shin, the mopper-up of Inchon, and Adm. Sohn, the South Korean Chief of Naval Operations, who happened to be present, were also to be decorated, in order, no doubt, to show no discrimination.[3]

Back at the road the proconsular party passed the previous day's bag of wrecked T-34s. "Considering they are Russian," said MacArthur, "these tanks are in the condition I desire them to be in." Then, to everyone's horror, Col. Murray asked the General whether, in that case, he would like to see the latest catch. Rifle fire was still sputtering below and the dead could be seen lying across the turrets of the burnt-out tanks. As Mac-Arthur, eagerly responding to this suggestion, strode on, a young officer came anxiously forward: "General," he said, "you can't come up here!" "Why?" asked MacArthur. "We've just knocked out six Red tanks at the top of this hill," replied the young man. "That was the proper thing to do," said the amused General. Beyond the pass, heavy firing could be heard as Roise's battalion advanced past Ascom City. Again Mac-Arthur climbed out of his jeep and, watching for a while, could see Kimpo Airfield clearly ahead. Finally, to Smith's relief, MacArthur agreed to drive back, having awarded the Silver Star to Murray before his departure. Before returning to the *Mount McKinley* the Commander in Chief saw some of the 671 prisoners in the 1st Division's stockade. Only afterwards was the apprehension of his staff justified when several NKPA were found hiding in the grass near the very spot from which Mac-Arthur had seen the burnt-out tanks and Kimpo. Unaware of the danger he had missed, the General summed up his visit as "a good sight for my old eyes."

The next two most evidently important tasks facing the U.N. at Inchon were the capture of Kimpo Airfield and of Seoul's suburb, Yongdungpo. There would have to be a divergence of attack here before the forces converged again for the final as-sault and capture of Seoul, which would also be approached from the southeast by Barr's infantrymen (of whom more in due course). Obviously the Kimpo task would go to the 5th Marines in the north and Yongdungpo to the 1st Marines. First, then, we will follow the advance to Kimpo.

On reaching the next phase line, 12 of the Division's 19-mile frontage would be the responsibility of the 5th Marines. Thus, Murray's advance was three-pronged; Maj. Kim's Korean Marine Corps Battalion was to attack due north, Roise's 2nd Battalion would move northeast by east, in the center of the Regiment, and have the main task of taking Kimpo itself, while Newton's 1st Battalion, taking the southern line, would proceed due eastward, almost to the extent of supporting Puller's advance on Yongdungpo. Such a mutually supporting front was, of course, in the proper military tradition. Taplett's 3rd Battalion was again in reserve. Soon after MacArthur's departure Murray returned to devote his attention to the deployment of his Regiment from the beachhead break-out towards Kimpo. They advanced in column; Roise leading, Newton next, Taplett off the road west of Ascom City, and the K.M.C. Battalion, which had already moved off at 0700 hours, advancing northward through Roise's original position. The main body of Murray's men started towards Kimpo at 0900 hours.

The advance through and around Ascom was deceptively easy, as will be seen in due course. The place was essentially an artificial town which had grown up around a shanty to cover an area of two square miles. Capt. Jaskilka's E Company worked its way around the southern limits of the town, encountering numerous pockets of NKPA resistance. He was assisted by A Company of the Tank Battalion, while a detached platoon of F Company, commanded by 2nd Lt. Tilton A. Anderson, found relatively little resistance in its advance through Ascom City itself, a task which it had regarded with some trepidation. Roise led his main column northward past the northern and left-hand flank of Ascom. Noon found him at the northeast corner of the town, trying to find the track which, evidently easier to spot from a height, was supposed to lead to Kimpo. Meanwhile, Newton's Company was advancing quickly along the road to Seoul and having a much easier time of it than the 1st Marines south of the road (presumably the luckless Sutter) who had encountered more determined NKPA troops. The enemy's axis of defense, however, was becoming more clearly established, as the most northern advance from Blue Beach was discovering to its discomfort.

In relation to MacArthur's earlier intention, it is interesting to note that the rice crop had mostly been harvested when Roise advanced through flat, featureless paddy fields towards Kimpo, occasionally coming across gardens of cabbages and leeks. Beyond Kimpo, two large hills which would be of future interest to the 5th Marines (Hills 131 and 125) dominated the left background. Between them lay a corridor, with shoulders and a few knolls arbitrarily named *Able* and *Baker*, which was the 2nd Battalion's initial objective. From here Roise would launch his final attack on Kimpo, three miles northward. A heartening feature as the men advanced was the spontaneous and genuine greeting they received from the local inhabitants.

While the so-called "Flying Column," composed of very weary Marines, continued to advance on Kimpo, the tanks found the route less suitable and had to change their line of approach to the Inchon-Kimpo road, approximately parallel to the 2nd Battalion's advance, two miles below it. 1st Lt. D. Pomeroy, commanding these tanks, was not the only man to secure more stable ground, for here he met his own Company Commander, Capt. Gerl M. English, whose tanks were accompanied by that extraordinary paramilitarist and *avant-garde* of Women's Lib, Marguerite Higgins (described by a Marine at Inchon as "the most beautiful press correspondent this writer has ever seen") who bet that she would be the first to set foot on Kimpo Airfield, a wager she gallantly lost to Capt. English. Tanks had come up to Roise's flank and swung north to support the 2nd Battalion's push towards Kimpo.

Meanwhile the Korean Marines and the battalion of the unfortunate Taplett, who had to undertake a great deal more unpleasant fighting than his reserve position indicated, had become caught up in a strange and unexpected duel with the enemy. The shooting was fierce and prolonged, owing to the NKPA's old trick of hiding until the front had pushed forward and then rising out of sewers and rat-infested drains with machine guns to unnerve the reserve troops. Eighteen NKPA were killed and Maj. Kim applied his mopping up operations even more stringently than before. Yet again Ascom City came under fire while Murray's command post was being stocked near the railway station. But 1st Lt. Nicholas A. Canzona * and his platoon of engineers were on hand, killing ten enemy and taking several prisoners. Maj. James D. Jordan had the greatest difficulty in landing A Battery, 11th Marines, and had to wade in as infantry. The chief opposition now came from the rear.

But Gen. Shepherd was a worried man. No news had come from Kimpo, and as he prepared for dinner on the *Mount McKinley* he knew quite well that MacArthur would ask him whether the airfield had yet been captured. Miss Higgins was not the only one who had to take cover from sporadic fire as the NKPA did its best to keep the Americans at bay; but eventually Roise's 2nd Battalion came level with the armor and before sunset on D+2 the airfield had fallen. Gen. Shepherd rushed into MacArthur's cabin in his pajamas to give him the news. At once the Commander in Chief was at his desk, informing the Pentagon.

But the enemy's strategy was becoming more coordinated and the night ahead contained something of a foretaste of the communists' stiffening resistance, although still sporadic by American standards. It was during the hour or two before dawn and during the early daylight hours of D+3 that their counterattacks became fiercer, evidently when they were aware of the strength and disposition of the various units which were now narrowly clinging on to Kimpo. Murray's deployment was as follows: Objective E, a shapeless hill feature on the road between Kimpo and the town of Sosa, about four miles to the southeast, was held by Newton's 1st Battalion, Taplett's 3rd Battalion, having extricated itself from the surprise resistance at Ascom, was still in reserve a mile back on the Ascom-Kimpo road, and Roise's 2nd Battalion was at Kimpo itself, sited around the southern sector of the airfield and its base installations. This last was the situation notably of F Company, 2nd Battalion, which included engineer and anti-tank platoons. E Company, 2nd Battalion, was over to the northeast where Lt. Deptula's platoon covered the northern approach to Soryu-li, a straggling brick-walled village. The Battalion's D Company, containing English's tanks and Roise's headquarters, held the west side of the main runway.

* Canzona was one of the two co-authors of the *Official History of the U.S. Marine Corps in Korea.*

The NKPA's deployment, as may be imagined from the pounding the airfield had received during the previous few days, was less easy to maintain against the constant anxiety of further aerial sorties which had done so much to undermine the morale of the defenders. Their forces consisted of the remnants of the 1st Air Division, the 107th Regiment, and the depleted 226th. The 877th Air Force Unit (whose task was to guard airfields) had put up slight resistance, but among its numerous casualties was its commanding officer, a figure who, as everyone who fought in Korea will know, was infinitely more important to his unit than his United Nations' equivalent because of the disparity of military intelligence between the few more senior officers and the rest. The Commanding Officer of the 107th is believed to have left his unit in a dangerous situation at the last minute.

The first enemy counterattack came at about 0300 hours in the area occupied by Deptula near Soryu-li. Down the road approaching the airfield came a reconnaissance of NKPA whose fieldcraft was evidently so inadequate that the Marines could hear them long before their shapes were actually visible on the road itself, like shoppers in the middle of a suburban precinct on a misty morning. As when the six tanks took such a roasting, the Marines remained silent while the North Koreans obligingly walked into a pocket of rifle and automatic fire, with the result that twelve NKPA soldiers lay dead before the rest managed to slip away into the darkness with bullets whining, cracking, and pinging around their ears. Three more communist probes were made during the next hour, each to be repulsed.

It was with the approach of dawn that the enemy decided to throw in its armor forcefully, which was a grave threat to Deptula who had no anti-tank weapons on hand. Thus, covering his withdrawal with mere rifle fire, he fell back on Capt. Jaskilka's better equipped E Company; while the T-34's, unaware of the Marines' deficiency, also turned back into the darkness. But shortly after Deptula's withdrawal, rifle fire onto Jaskilka's position came from the area Deptula had occupied. It was several minutes before the Americans realized that this was not from a bunch of trigger-happy members of D Company, but from some NKPA soldiers who had infiltrated Deptula's position during the night with evidently better fieldcraft than those who had strolled down the road a little earlier. Whether or not it was intentional, this disparity of military standard was strange and almost sinister. The brunt of the attack was borne by the platoon commanded by 2nd Lt. Charles Christiensen which repulsed the enemy, owing largely to the mortar fire put down by Sgt. Marvin Eggersluss and a grenade charge by Cpl. William House who was killed shortly before the enemy withdrew.

Southeast of Kimpo an enemy demolition squad had been stopped by one of F Company's outposts, and later another probe was halted at the same place, where a bridge crossed the Ascom City road.

But perhaps the biggest counterattack was that foreseen by Capt. Fenton's B Company from the high ground, Objective E, south of Kimpo where about 200 NKPA soldiers were seen passing across the enemy's front. Roise was informed and the Marines held their fire. Here observers of the 11th Marines and the U.S. Infantry watched action in the Inchon beachhead for the first time. When the Marines' pocket, penetrating eastward, was sufficiently full, Roise's and Newton's mortar bombs whistled down on the surprised enemy, accompanied by fire from F Company's riflemen and Fenton's enfilade. Except for a slight protraction of the engagement by an isolated platoon under 2nd Lt. James E. Harrell, who used white phosphorus incendiary rockets, it was all over within minutes.

With the first light of D+3, Pershings were called up to secure the perimeter of the airfield and later the 2nd Battalion consolidated its hold on Kimpo, Soryu-li, and other villages. Meanwhile, Lt. Smith's D Company advanced unopposed on Hill 131 which overlooks the Han River. Down toward the stream, a decisive breakthrough of *Chromite*, they moved in a mood of both apprehension and confidence. At least Alexander had reached his Euphrates! Now that Kimpo had been secured the Americans could land not only their Corsairs for rocket attacks on Seoul, but the heavy bombers and all the equipment they would need to cross the Han. Although Yongdungpo had yet to be captured, the Americans could now begin the build up for the final objective of the Inchon landing. What Churchill had, on another occasion, called "the end of the beginning" was imminent.[4]

CHAPTER SEVEN

Anxiety in the Beachhead

Thus far, the invaders had strengthened their position with the passing of every hour, and although their hold on Inchon and the country beyond was never in serious doubt during *Operation Chromite*, there now followed that period common to many outstanding amphibious operations when the element of surprise has been totally eroded and the enemy is able to make better plans for its defense. The Allies found this particularly at Anzio, the Americans at an early stage on the Omaha Beach in Normandy and the British and Canadians at Caen a little later. And where Gallipoli and Maida witnessed the same phenomenon the former resulted in evacuation and the latter in a triumph which, evidence of skill and courage, owed everything to the timely arrival of the British 20th Foot. And so it happened, although less perceptibly at Inchon, where the Americans, having swept the enemy aside with ridiculous ease, now faced the North Koreans who had been rushed to the front with greater intelligence of the situation. The momentum was difficult to sustain. But with Kimpo captured and the Han reached there was no fear that anything approaching a reversal would occur, nor did it; but the United Nations had to work to a strict time schedule, imposed by the elements as well as the durability of the Eighth Army, and they could afford no interference in the beachhead to upset the advance to Seoul. But as the Marines pressed on towards Yongdungpo they were relieved to hear that they would be supported on their southern flank by the 7th Infantry Division, U.S. Army, and that there was evidence that Gen. Walker's Army was at last making efforts to stir from its atrophied positions around Pusan which, after all, was the essential purpose of the exercise. But, as if to counter any anxiety that might be developing in the beachhead, allied spirits were lifted as the Corsairs duly took advantage of Murray's victory at Kimpo.

But we must give the enemy full credit where it was due, however slender. At about the moment when the NKPA's tanks were being strafed early on September 17th, the North Korean Air Force made its only strike throughout the operation. At about 0555 hours two YAK-3s and a Stormovik IL-10, a Russian fighter and fighter-bomber respectively, made straight for Adm. Struble's flagship, the *Rochester*, each aircraft dropping four 100-lb. bombs, all but one of which fell into the water close by. The other glanced off the ship's aircraft crane but did not explode. The *Rochester*, rather curiously, was caught quite unawares, and could only reply with a volley of eight .30 rifle fire. Five thousands yards astern of the flagship was HMS *Jamaica*, the bridge and topside of which were raked with machine gun and cannon fire which killed one and injured two of the ship's company. But, fired with more warning, the 4-in. pom-pom shells let fly with great accuracy and speed, and the Stormovik plunged into the sea. As the *Jamaica*'s Capt. J. S. C. Salter R.N. remarked, ". . . foolhardy of them to go for two cruisers when they had a choice of transports and freighters galore."[1] But with Kimpo captured the North Korean Air Force was greatly restricted in its aerial ambitions; indeed, with the airfield came a small haul consisting of a Yak and two more Stormoviks, others having been destroyed or damaged by the retreating NKPA. An undamaged Yak thereafter received U.S. Air Force markings and deserted the enemy! It may even have been the assailant of D+2.

The two most senior members of the U.S. Marine Air Wing at Inchon were Maj. Gen. Field Harris, commanding the 1st Marine Aircraft Wing and Brig. Gen. Thomas J. Cushman, commanding the Tactical Air Command, X Corps. While it was necessary to make immediate use of Kimpo, Harris did not intend to do so at the cost of those afloat on the carriers, but by increasing his strength from supplies in Japan. Cushman, of course, was directly answerable to Almond, the X Corps

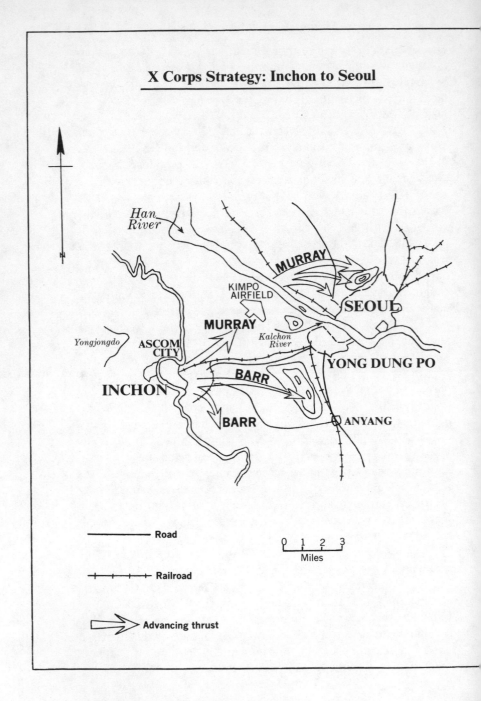

X Corps Strategy: Inchon to Seoul

Han River

MURRAY

KIMPO AIRFIELD

MURRAY

Kalchon River

SEOUL

Yongjongdo

ASCOM CITY

YONG DUNG PO

INCHON

BARR

BARR

ANYANG

——————— Road

+—+—+—+ Railroad

0 1 2 3
Miles

Advancing thrust

Commander, who approved the decision to use this command; in fact the headquarters and service elements of MAG-33 (Marine Air Group) to strike at Seoul from Kimpo as from D+4, September 19th. Until then the airfield was out of bounds to Corsairs, although, on some specious pretext, one did manage to land from the *Badoeng Strait*, and its pilot, Lt. John V. Haines, was sternly rebuked by the generals. But on returning to the carrier he was welcomed aboard and suitably toasted by his messmates for having made the first shore landing at Inchon.

Stern rivalry between the services under Bradley's overall command was particularly evident at Inchon where the U.S. Marines, despite their fine reputation, were fighting hard to justify themselves and disabuse forever the Joint Chiefs of Staff of the stigma which had been attached to them by Louis Johnson. It might even be said, looking at the situation objectively and from the standpoint both of time and personal allegiance, that the U.S. Marines at this particular moment had a chip on their shoulders when it came to a comparison of usefulness between them and the U.S. Army or Air Force (or the U.S. Army Air Force, as they had been before MacArthur, supporting the cause of Gen. Billy Mitchell, was the chief impulse in dividing the two commands). MacArthur might have been a soldier, but he had made such use of every branch of every service in the Pacific, particularly the Marine Corps, that, like Odysseus's Athene, he was all things to all men. It was natural, however, that his Chief of Staff should also be a senior U.S. Army officer; but without MacArthur's kudos, and in view of his being placed in command of X Corps, Marine criticism was likely to persist. As I have already noted, this officer was Maj. Gen. Edward M. Almond, and his being answerable only to the Commander in Chief in all matters, whether as Chief of Staff or of X Corps, placed him in an invidious position. It was an error of judgment, albeit not of Almond's personal ability, for which MacArthur alone was responsible. But, of course, it was convenient to have the man privy to both tasks. Mention will be made of the position in the overall assessment at the end, but already we have found one issue for which Almond's Marine colleagues criticized him. Others will appear as the operation proceeds. His was an unenviable task.

This particular criticism concerned the restoration of life to Kimpo which, it was alleged by a senior Marine critic of the General, was vitiated by X Corps' poor logistics. Briefly, it was asserted that X Corps staff did not put their transport ashore soon enough to operate the port and that this delay was robbing the Marine Air Wing of fuel which should have gone straight to Cushman's Corps Marine Air Wing, a defect which involved Almond's Chief of Staff (Brig. Gen. Hodes) having to make *ad hoc* arrangements with the Far East Air Force to fly sufficient fuel for the build-up of aircraft on the airfield. By this means, 3,338 tons of all classes of supply reached Kimpo for operation of the air base, while only 1,450 tons reached Kimpo from the X Corps pipeline at Inchon.

But other logistical deficiencies were also attributed to X Corps Command. Whereas the organization of Kimpo (as distinct from its flight operations) was the responsibility of the 5th Air Force, it appears that MAG-33 was landed with this duty because the Air Force had approved no ambulances, crash trucks, refuellers, or water purification units, and when the Air Force's communication center arrived it was deficient of the correct cryptographic publications and equipment. It seems, in fact, as if the Marines undertook the re-equipment and tidying up of the airfield for serviceability in addition to their normal military duties.

But while these domestic issues tended to create disunity, they had to be overlooked when compared with the overall task of securing the Inchon beachhead. The main Pyongyang-Pusan road and railway, to the front of the perimeter, was still in enemy hands and with the passing of every day, the NKPA could make contingency plans to transfer a large number of men to the vulnerable southern sector of the Inchon beachhead where Puller's men still had only a tenuous control of the right flank. There was concern in the beachhead, both for the military survival of this vulnerable sector and for the proper logistical function of X Corps. They were to be short-lived worries, but in so finely balanced an operation there was no room for error. More acrimony was to persist between the Marines and the Army as the Corps grouped for its final thrust around Seoul. To the objective eye it does seem that the

Marines were the more unnecessarily critical of the two. The feud was the only sour note in an otherwise wonderfully cohesive operation. MacArthur seemed hardly to be aware of its existence and assumed that everyone (at least among the military in Korea) saw *Chromite* in the same simple, straightforward, and unpartisan way as he did.

CHAPTER EIGHT

Yongdungpo and the Passage of the Han

For the first time in 56 years, since 1894 when protection was required of the American legation in Seoul during the Japanese advance into the capital of Korea, American Marines were heading eastward along the Inchon-Seoul road. But this time, swift though the invasion had been, the Marines moved with more caution against a more mysterious enemy. Although, as the tank battle near Ascom City had shown, the communists could not hope to retake Inchon, they could protect Seoul by holding the invaders for as long as possible at a prepared position at the capital's main suburb, Yongdungpo, on the western flank of the city. This, as we have seen, would be the objective of the 1st Marines. While the 5th Marines had captured Kimpo and were preparing to cross the Han on Seoul's northern flank, Puller's men downstream would go straight for Yongdungpo from the west and so over the river and into the center of the capital. The southeastern sector, as we will see, would become the responsibility of Maj. Gen. Barr's 7th Infantry Division, but only after some unfortunate internecine squabbling in X Corps.

Puller launched his advance on September 17th. His plan, as described in Chapter 6, was that Sutter's 2nd Battalion would initially advance along the main road, then into the high ground around Hill 208, south of Ascom and the road. Behind Sutter, also prepared to move initially to his right, was Ridge's 3rd Battalion and B Company of the Tank Battalion under Capt. Bruce F. Williams. Well to the south, covering the vul-

116

nerable right flank of the Division, was Hawkins' 1st Battalion and Houghton's Reconnaissance Company.

Sutter began his advance at 0700 hours, at the precise moment when Shin's South Korean Marines were moving northward from Murray's beachhead on the extreme left. Sutter advanced easily along the road, while his D and F Companies, south of the road, approached Hill 208. The NKPA, which was attempting to resist him from the hills, was duly engaged by the 11th Marines, commanded by an able gunner in Lt. Col. Merritt Adelman who was amply equipped with 105 mm guns which he used to good effect. The 11th Marines, commanded by Col. James H. Browser, had landed on Blue Beach on D+1 under the advance guard of Lt. Col. Jim Crowe.

The progress of Ridge's battalion was suddenly held up when its E Company, under 1st Lt. Johnny L. Carter, was obstructed by a roadblock west of the mud village of Mahang-ri which itself was on the right flank of well-defended positions on Hill 208. Carter outflanked the roadblock and assaulted the enemy from a flank, inflicting 20 fatal casualties on the enemy. As the Marines assaulted the village they were held up by several determined NKPA, well covered by a hedgerow. Carter remembered the incident well. "Every time we threw three or four grenades into the hedge we received six or seven back in return." [1] That it was Ridge's and not Sutter's men who received this resistance is explained by the fact that Puller decided to effect deep penetration with his tanks and attached them to Ridge, whose men embarked in amtracs to join the tanks along the road. Meanwhile, Sutter's battalion moved over to the left flank, north of the road. Ridge, then, with the swifter means of advance, did not cross his start-line until 1000 hours and was thus caught early by the resistance at Mahang-ri. Soon the tanks were up to assist Carter. A Pershing was at once in action against an unsuspecting T-34 (equipped with an 85-mm gun) and the 90-mm cannon of the Marine tank soon destroyed the ponderous Russian vehicle. This was followed immediately by another explosion when a house, evidently well stocked with high explosives, was unwittingly touched off by the gun of another Pershing; and twelve NKPA prisoners, on their way to the rear, were among the victims. Mahang-ri did not fall until mid-afternoon, but Puller was still in a hurry and preferred to continue the tactics of assault rather than favor attrition. The momentum had to be maintained, and MacArthur himself had told his commanders that at no time were the Marines to adopt the habit of digging in and slogging it out unless ingenuity was completely outwitted. He could have found no more resolute a disciple than Puller who had always favored swift advance.

The colonel would need to maintain this admirable intention throughout the next few days if he were not to get bogged down by the enemy who was likely to delay his advance in various degrees of strength throughout the line of advance. Soon he encountered another difficulty. About half a mile further on a ridge cut across the road where it was flanked on both sides by high ground; so that it lay, in effect, in a defile. Some NKPA retreated swiftly from Mahang-ri, others came up from the next village (Sosa), and anti-tank guns were suitably deployed. The enemy had time to prepare itself here because the Pershings had ignominiously run out of gasoline and had to be refueled halfway between Mahang-ri and the ridge while tank commanders muttered unmentionable things. Capt. Westover later wrote: "While we sat awaiting gasoline the NKPAs had every opportunity to fortify that area beyond the defiles and outside Sosa—*which they did!*" [2] So emboldened, in fact, did the enemy become that they fixed bayonets and charged at Carter's company in the wide paddy fields which approached the defile, but had cause to regret their enthusiasm. The charging infantry were shot down like moving targets, becoming conveniently larger, on a rifle range. The North Koreans had failed to realize that the American, through history, has never been more certain of himself than when his eye is behind a rifle, stetson or not.

But while Westover's men were working through the defile the enemy let off everything they had, rifle fire, mortars, and anti-tank guns, at them and the leading Pershings, commanded by 2nd Lt. Bryan J. Cummings. While the Marines were now prone, the engine of Cummings' tank went dead on him and he became isolated amidst a horde of yelling NKPA. He managed momentarily to open his hatch and grab an exposed Marine who had been concealed behind the turret—an act of charity rewarded by the man's becoming hysterical as smoke filled the tank, until one of the crew quietened him with his fist. The Pershing was eventually saved by another which machine gunned the enemy crawling over the hull of Cummings' vehicle, but not before a grenade had been stuffed into an aperture and caused some injury. An airstrike by five Corsairs cleared the enemy, and the Marines pressed on, but only towards other anti-tank guns which blew a track off Cummings' ill-fated war horse. When the Marines reached the crest of the ridge the enemy retreated east to Sosa, leaving 250 dead, 70 prisoners and six guns. The Marines had suffered one fatal and 34 wounded casualties.

D+3 was quiet, but support on to the high ground came from the sea when HMS *Kenya* fired over 300 6-in. shells on Hill 123, east of Sosa and north of the road. Now Ridge moved left again, through Sutter's position, and Sosa was captured with few casualties. Meanwhile, for Hawkins' 1st Battalion, the advance was going smoothly. Consolidation east of Sosa was the automatic drill while the 5th Marines approached the left bank of the Han from Kimpo, about seven miles northwest of Seoul.

Now the Army's detachment began to arrive when Col. Charles E. Beauchamp's 32nd Infantry, vanguard of Maj. Gen. Barr's 7th Division, landed at Inchon on D+3. They waited while the rest of the Division disembarked and were able to cover the exposed right flank of the 1st Marines which had caused Smith and Puller so much concern. Next morning the 32nd Regiment would relieve Hawkins' 1st Battalion, 1st Marines, and the Marine Reconnaissance Company. There seems to have been some delay here, caused by lack of liaison between the Marines and soldiers, attributable by the Marines to the X Corps command structure.

Barr was fully ashore by D+4, and when, the next day, the 31st Regiment arrived all was ready for the Army to join the pursuit. This enabled Almond to feel that he could handle affairs personally, and he was anxious to capture Seoul not later than September 25th, 90 days after the communist invasion.

Back at Yongdungpo, Puller's commanders were examining the task ahead. The town was (and presumably still is) surrounded by a moat and several ridges between Kimpo and

Yongdungpo, culminating in Hill 118 (*Paeksok* to the Koreans) which threateningly overlooked the road. Many defenders of Kimpo had fled to this area from the 5th Marines and the immediate future was uncertain for both the pursuers and the pursued. To tackle the situation Hawkins was ordered northward to help the 5th Marines capture the feature and the two small twin hills, 80 and 85, which lie astride the approach to Yongdungpo. These had to be captured by any force attempting to take Yongdungpo from the north and west. This was all part of a plan to move the Marines northward to assist Murray and for the 7th Division to spread out in their wake, while, at the same time, securing their flank.

Newton was ordered by Murray to attack Hill 118 next day from country which he held between Paeksok and Kimpo. But as B and C companies, 5th Marines, were about to launch their offensive, 500 NKPA sprang an assault on C Company with small arms and mortar fire. They evidently intended to retake Kimpo, having moved during the night from Seoul along the Yongdungpo-Kimpo road, below the Marines' positions farther north. The Marines' supporting artillery (1st Battalion, 11th Marines) were partly on hand, but Pederson managed to call in an air strike by VMF-214.

Capt. Fenton, unscathed by the enemy, was ordered by Newton to take Hill 118, and he duly assaulted the communists in the flank and rear. At enormous speed Fenton carried the advance so that the hill was reached, without a casualty, by about 1100 hours on D+4. What had begun as a communist offensive had ended as an outstanding tactical defeat of the NKPA. Fenton's B Company on the high ground held fire while Pederson smashed the enemy between his C Company and Fenton's position. The enemy seemed habitually to lack the subtle art of sound warfare, as Fenton wrote, "Once again the enemy had failed to watch his flank and was caught with his pants down." [3] The North Koreans, unaware of B Company's position, became so confused that they lost 300 dead and 150 prisoners.* Throughout the afternoon, particularly in the latter half, New-

---

* It was rarely possible to estimate the communists' losses in wounded casualties.

ton's battalions held Paeksok and its two approach hillocks, 80 and 85. To his assistance came Hawkins, relieved by the Army, although the primitive roads had held up his advance.

Now the enemy withdrew to the fringe of Yongdungpo itself, from which they directed heavy machine gun and anti-tank rifle fire on the captured hills. David Rees, in his book *Korea: The Limited War*, may have written ruefully about the disastrous effect of war on the poor third world countries, at the mercy of power blocs which have, on the one hand, manpower, and on the other weaponry; but on such an occasion as this it was the supremacy of the weaponry which managed to speed war away from the miserable people of Yongdungpo. Up came the howitzers of Lt. Col. Ransom M. Wood's 1/11th Marines, firing 85 105-mm shells, and down came the enemy's fortifications. Also, much to the Marine engineers' anger, down came a section of the bridge when, next day, a shell fired at Seoul fell short. By evening on D+4 Hawkins arrived in the area, and he sent A Company under Capt. Robert H. Barrow ahead to Paeksok. But Barrow arrived first on Hills 80 and 85 —forward positions which he was anxious to secure as a priority; but Hawkins would not allow Barrow and Fenton to hold them jointly through the night and he ordered Barrow to move on, as arranged. The captain was vindicated when, before dawn next day, the NKPA attacked. They swarmed over the features, dug in, and despite U.S. Marine air strikes the 1st Marines had to fight hard to win the two hills back again.

Ridge's 3rd Battalion, meanwhile advanced northwest from "Shrapnel Hill" and the Inchon–Yongdungpo road to win Sinjong-ni ("Look-Out Hill"), similar high ground south of 118. This held a good view over Yongdungpo and even across to Seoul itself. Harassed and sniped at from the hills, like a stage coach passing through Apache country, Ridge's men pressed on over four dusty miles, and by dusk they held "Look-Out Hill."

Sutter, advancing along the main road, however, was meeting stronger resistance. Artillery smashed one of the leading tanks of C Company, 1st Battalion under Capt. Richard M. Taylor, and the Marines were completely pinned down short of the knolls which abut the road. Six Corsairs from VMF-214 dropped napalm in considerable quantity over the entire suspected position of the NKPA, but still the enemy resisted. 1st Lt. George A. Babe showed great courage in leading his men through a minefield, marking each mine and then blowing it. But then every natural obstacle, and many unnatural ones, that could be found hampered the advance, until Puller, enraged by the 32nd Infantry's continued absence from the south flank, broke the unwritten code and ordered his men to advance across the Army's line of approach, for reasons of self-protection. He did not realize that Beauchamp was not to move off until the next morning.

Sutter thrust on with D Company, tanks, and an umbrella of Corsairs. A tankdozer went in and was disposing of the road blocks, when the earth shook, the vehicle lifted momentarily from the ground, and a wheel spun across the track. Another mine had done its work. Once again Babe went in and did his task with great coolness while the tanks stood back. Then up went the mines and on went the tanks, crewmen no doubt savoring the skill of battle with fervent prayer. The Marines did take Hill 146 before dusk, but the NKPA had put up a great fight, soon to be renewed with even more aggression, while Sutter (to indicate the toughness of *his* foes) took only five prisoners. Next day, D+5, was to be the harshest so far.

In the shadow and optical illusion of early dawn an NKPA battalion, with five T-34's, prepared to strike the Marines on the road from Yongdungpo. In they whined, but Sutter held his fire until a vicious reply of a machine gun to a challenging call set off the action. A communist ammunition truck splayed pyrotechnics over the awakening country as it struck a mine, one of Babe's returns. Carter's E Company took the punishment for this, but the Marines closed in around the enemy and Sutter tightened the ring. Carter returned fire. The NKPA's tanks which tried to retreat ran into D and F Companies, while others were trapped by Adelman's battalion of 155 mm howitzers and by the 96th Field Artillery under Lt. Col. Richard T. Knowles.

At this moment, the bazookaman, P.F.C. Monegan, whose gallantry was recorded on the occasion when the NKPA lost six tanks and 200 men just over the Inchon coastal ridge (he wielding a rocket launcher), ran down on the T-34's and disposed of two more tanks at suicidal range after a miss, before he was killed by machine gun fire. He did not live to learn that he had been awarded the Medal of Honor and would, no doubt, be amazed and mystified to know that, still today, children in a neighboring village adorn a photograph of him with flowers on September 20th every year. Cpl. Cheek, Pvt. Perkins and others will be recalled by those who witnessed the heroic fighting early that morning. As the sun rose the Marines could see the carnage wrought among the North Koreans. More than 300 NKPA lay dead in the most hideous postures and in very unlikely places. High explosive can hurl the earth about, so that if tanks stood on their turrets it was hardly surprising to see corpses like dead cats, tossed into the grasping branches of the sparse foliage.

Hawkins, who from his rear position might have done better to heed the warning of the officers on Hills 80 and 85, now had to retake the hills. Capt. Robert P. Wray of C Company would operate the plan and Maj. William L. Bates, Jr., commanding Weapons Company, would cover the assaulting Marines from Hill 118. First, Wray had to take a village below Paeksok, and although he was well covered by both Bates and the enfilade fire of the Marines already on Hill 118, the village appeared to contain at least a company of NKPA who were not finally flushed out until noon. This had involved two assaults which meant complicated fire and movement ("envelopment") which the NKPA commander on Hill 85 had watched with interest. It was unfortunate that Wray could not have attacked both hills simultaneously, rather than give one of them a preview before turning his attention to the other. Thus the assault on Hill 85 was an even bloodier affair. The enemy was deployed in a horseshoe formation, well concealed, and gave the impression in the first assault that resistance would be negligible. Only as the Marines approached the top did they receive fire from three directions, and it was with the greatest heroism that they pushed on to the top. 2nd Lt. John Guild, although hit in the chest by the machine gun fire, continued to encourage his men forward while he lay propped on one arm until he fell dead; 2nd Lt. Henry A. Commiskey led his men to the very top, handing his automatic weapon to a man whose rifle had jammed and taking on the enemy with his fists. He was the third recipient of the Medal of Honor. Capt. Wray's radioman, unknown to his preoccupied commander, lay seriously wounded, yet still kept Lt. Col. Hawkins in touch with the progress of the battle.

Now the Marines and the 7th Divison would have to begin to pull out all the stops. The element of surprise was as old as the Han Dynasty. The fights for Yongdungpo and Seoul would prove that, in the last resort, even the most technically efficient military force in the world would have to rely upon the stamina and courage of its individual members, qualities which themselves are the reward of fine training and *esprit de corps*.

Now, with Hills 80, 85, and 118 in the Marines' hands, and with their control of the roads connecting Yongdungpo with Kimpo and Sosa, *Chromite* was beginning to approach its climax. With the capture of Yongdungpo and the passage of the Han imminent, there remained only the seizure of Seoul and, with the main north-south artery cut and morale greatly boosted, the breakout of the Eighth Army from Pusan. Upon the success of the next few days MacArthur had staked his whole reputation.

But first it was essential to ensure that Seoul and its suburb were surrounded, as far as possible, by an iron ring to the west, reaching around to the north and south as far and as fast as time would allow. Sustaining several fatal and wounded casualties, Col. Beauchamp (box minefields notwithstanding) had approached from the south and had reached Tongchok Mountain overlooking the Kalchon River, about 1,500 yards south of Sutter's command post. Beauchamp's own vehicle had ploughed through a covey of mines, his driver had been killed, his radio operator wounded, the jeep wrecked, and he himself unharmed but baptized. Beauchamp had a formidable strength of NKPA to his front which disturbed Puller. It was with further criticism of liaison with X Corps Headquarters that the Marines eventually discovered, after seven hours when it had long been dark, that permission was received for the Marine artillery to soften the enemy, muzzle flash notwithstanding. But, as it turned out, this would be of little concern since the 11th Marines had already turned Yongdungpo, containing the 87th

NKPA Regiment for garrison defense, into a blazing furnace. The night of D+5 was one of anticipation in the mind of every U.N. serviceman at Inchon.

Already that day MacArthur, with Shepherd, Struble, Almond, and senior staff officers, had toured the C.P.'s. Gen. Barr was relieved to feel that he had at least two regiments ashore and in position up to the boundary line with the 1st Marines on the Inchon-Seoul road. Almond was also pleased. With the disparity between marines and soldiers favoring the Army he felt more confident in his relations with Gen. Smith and would imminently assume command of the X Corps ashore.

But how was the enemy deployed to defend Yongdungpo? Few doubted that the first real battle would take place here. The town was pear-shaped, and with trained manpower at a premium the NKPA chose to defend what they considered to be three essential sectors of the perimeter; the northern apex at the confluence of the Han with the Kalchon (notably opposite the high ground occupied by the 5th Marines between Hills 80 and 85), about 2,500 yards farther south along the eastern branch of the Kalchon, and along a 2,000-yard stretch immediately southeast of the Inchon-Seoul road opposite the 7th Division. The maze of buildings was such as to make the town's defense a protracted affair if it were carefully carried out and although the enemy lacked trained soldiers there were many thousand who were capable of discharging a guerrilla warfare with large quantities of arms and ammunition at their disposal. They were also plentifully supplied with tanks, but mercifully not tank crews. Densely built though Yongdungpo was, the enemy failed to take the advantage which this afforded. A conurbation of such shape would have to be defended in depth, each sector mutually supporting. It was just no use to suppose that because one could cover the critical axes of approach with adequate firepower the defense was impregnable. In fact, a road entered the town almost halfway between the two more northern lines of defense, and it was both a weakness at this point of the perimeter and a failure to cover this aperture from behind that was the defenders' chief tactical failure.

The battle for Yongdungpo began at 0630 hours on D+6 under the immediate Marine command of Colonel Puller. Naturally, battalions were sent from sectors they already held on the town's outskirts, with Ridge's 3rd Battalion in reserve on Look Out Hill, affording support for both the other battalions. Hawkins, from the hills, assaulted the north of the town and Sutter, from the south, crossed the western Kalchon at the point where the 7th Division should have been adjacent to the Marines.

The bridge here was tested by engineers, and on its being pronounced safe the tanks of C Company advanced with the Marines of D and F. Corsairs of VMF-214 softened up the defenders ahead. F Company moved down the road and D fanned out to the left towards Ridge's reserve which, in fact, was right on the start line. As General Smith noted, Puller had the aggressive habit of keeping his reserve units virtually in the front line where most regimental commanders would normally site their observation posts. From the ridge, Kuroi-ni, the enemy's artillery put down accurate fire on the advancing Marines; but the 32nd Infantry, in whose line of advance the ridge lay, were not, as had been supposed, in position, and time was wasted while an alternative counterattack was being considered. Infuriated, Puller ordered Sutter to bring up his reserve company and the Marines' 4.2-in. mortars (known as four deuces) to deal with the enemy. One cannot help feeling that the relations between the Marines and the Army were contrived, and that Colonel Puller, of all the Marine commanders, was trying to maximize the difficulties. But worse was to come. Sutter faced the nucleus of the NKPA's 87th Regiment on Kuroi-ni, and, despite MacArthur's preference for the chase, he had to dig in. Carter's men were pinned down in the stream's bottom by machine gun fire, and on his right could use only the railway embankment for concealment as he tried to push some of his men forward. But eventually he was pulled back and took cover with D Company, the left assault company, around a suitably placed brick factory. This withdrawal involved an air strike by Corsairs from the Badoeng Strait which was so successful that Carter could afterward report: "We crossed the open space to our rear without a casualty." [4] It is some evidence of the enemy's ferocity at Yongdungpo that this should have been the Marines' first withdrawal in *Chromite*.

D Company also had a tough fight north of the road, so that

Puller had to rely more than usual on tank support. One company under Capt. Welby Cronk was stopped only a hundred yards short of the ancient ramparts and could not move. Disappointed by his lack of progress the 1st Marines' commander now had to trim his sails and weather the storm. All would eventually be well provided Puller did not have to surrender captured territory. The plan had to be changed and Puller lost no time in ordering up Ridge's reserve battalion. With MacArthur's warning very much in mind, and no doubt wishing to live up to his own reputation, Puller conceived the brave idea of an advance by Ridge from Look Out Hill, across the Kalchon, and up the eastern stream. The 3rd Battalion duly set off at 1530 hours and since little artillery support could be sought, Ridge had to rely almost entirely on his own weapons company. Consequently a machine gun duel, which smacked more of former days, rattled out from both sides until the battalion was able to cross and push Westover's and Fisher's companies upstream to the bridge which carried the main road westward towards Inchon. In this rather insecure position, on the angle of the east bank of the Kalchon and the exit of the main road, Ridge secured his battalion as far as possible and awaited nocturnal vicissitudes. The wounded were carried out across the bridge to the rear under cover of darkness, but one of the company commanders (Capt. Bland) was able to stay with his men despite suffering 40 wounds.

But now, with the situation barely contained, the Marines were able to exploit the weakness in the NKPA's defense. The opportunity fell to Capt. Barrow's A Company, 1st Marines, to drive into the heart of Yongdungpo while its comrades were being held up by fierce resistance to his north and south. Hawkins issued an order to thrust down the road from Kimpo at 0730; Barrow moved off Paeksok, across the rough country towards the Kalchon, and into the heart of Yongdungpo. During the night Bland's B Company had moved downstream from the bridge, forward and to the right of Barrow's thrust. Supported on both flanks by Marines who had managed to draw abreast with the root of his advance, and by the reinforced 11th Battalion, Barrow accelerated towards the Han. So deep and so sudden was the battalion's penetration that radio communication was lost and neither Puller nor Hawkins could say specifically where the men were. Past a school, the town hall, and a clay pipe factory, over a slight rise which might have afforded a good defensive position, Barrow drove his attenuating wedge, heedless of the danger that he might reach a point where the enemy could consider encirclement from the west. But only one man seems to have been more surprised than Puller, the commander of the NKPA 87th Regiment. When his patrols stumbled across the intruding Marines, either by accident or design, they were dealt with as thoroughly as a bunch of cattle rustlers being taken to the sheriff's office. Three such columns were shot down, one of them so unaware that it was actually singing a tub-thumping revolutionary song. When Barrow reached a dike, well into eastern Yongdungpo, he was approached by three tank patrols (one at less than 20 yards), but by good aiming and clever bluff his men managed to scare them off. Barrow spent two nights in the town before the 1st and 3rd Battalions advanced eastward at 0800 hours on D+7. Why Hawkins did not support Barrow's company from a rear flank on D+6, or why the enemy did not attack him in greater strength the present author, at least, cannot understand and can find no adequate explanation. But the Marines had taken the only chance open to them and had turned a battle of attrition into an overwhelming victory.

Gen. Barr had an ill-rewarding arrival at Inchon. The Army's first great achievement in the south was to cut the Suwon-Anyang corridor, when Lt. Col. Charles M. Mount committed many young and inexperienced soldiers of his 2nd Battalion, 32nd Infantry, to action for the first time on D+6, September 21st. But the Army and the Marines Corps even failed to agree over the occurrence of an event on the ground, namely the bombing of the enemy's artillery pieces at Kuroi-ni by Lt. Norman Vining's Corsairs. Puller complained to Barr that the Army was refusing to acknowledge the existence of Marine air strikes. If such evident fundamentals could not be agreed upon, the situation was decidedly unhealthy. Neither Almond's deputy, Gen. Hodes, nor Col. Beauchamp could see the alleged activity from a position with a commanding view eastwards. Nor could they see alleged artillery support. Yet Sutter's battalion had undoubtedly been under heavy fire from the ridge. The explanation could have been that while both arms were right, and no incorrect map reading could be deduced, or indeed expected from such experienced servicemen, maps of disparate scale were being used. If so, it was an extraordinary error in an operation otherwise planned to the finest detail. Little wonder that Sutter was so heavily shelled!

The 32nd Infantry next took Suwon, but not without a misunderstanding which involved the death of a senior staff officer, Lt. Col. Henry Hampton, as a result of his openly approaching several T-34's which he had supposed in the dark to be Pershings. His aim had been to go ahead personally to coordinate operations against the town, but his zeal was misplaced and several soldiers narrowly escaped the same fate. With its capture came the use of Suwon Airfield which could carry the heavy R5D's. The 31st Regiment reached its Phase Line F, the ultimate objective of X Corps on this sector of the front in *Chromite*, and while Barr had been dilatory in the north, on the 1st Marines' southern boundary, he had moved swiftly southward to encourage Walker.

Meanwhile, from various parts of the world, came a unit that would be reconstituted as the 7th Marines under Col. ("Litz the Blitz") Litzenberg. A piecemeal unit, it consisted of reservists from Camp Pendleton, the East Coast 2nd Marine Division, the 6th Marines, an artillery battalion of the 10th Marines and the 3/6th Marines which had sailed from the Mediterranean to Japan where it became the 3/7th. The 7th Marines reached Inchon on D+5. Deployment followed at once. The 2nd Battalion was placed under Hill 131, north of Kimpo, the 3rd Battalion was two miles farther south, while the 1st had the non-combatant role of unloading supplies at Inchon.

As the offensive advanced inland the naval support was naturally of decreasing value. The 8-in. guns of the cruisers could fire 12 to 15 miles and were now of marginal use, and while for a reason unknown to the author the great USS *Missouri,* on which MacArthur had received the Japanese surrender, was not used in Korea (and yet was riding at anchor in Inchon harbor, where MacArthur paid it a sentimental visit), its guns could have assisted the land forces up to 20 miles inland.

The decline of naval assistance meant that the time had come for Almond to assume command of X Corps ashore. The General now began his new responsibility, one of his first aims being to restore to the Corps the cohesion between soldiers and Marines, and the consequent damage to discipline and morale which all the American forces were suffering in varying degrees. There was one enemy, one objective, and one unit for the Corps' achievement. And Almond had been appointed the one leader. He duly set up his own headquarters in the MSTS *Buckner,* and as he and MacArthur arrived again in Korea, Puller and Murray were converging on Seoul and the marines were poised to cross the Han.

Almond was in an extraordinary position. Experienced as a senior staff officer, although of course with much combat service, his staff duties would now have to be subordinated to his personal leadership at a crucial stage in the operation which he had helped to plan but at no stage yet to command. MacArthur did have a temporary stand-in, but suddenly to redelegate someone's staff work is never very satisfactory for short periods of time, and Brig. Gen. Hodes must have had a thankless task. Although the United States forces had reached a natural barrier the momentum of their drive had to be maintained, so that they could not sit back and take stock of the situation while their new commander took over. The author can think of no comparable situation, the only conceivable exception being the quasi-executive command played by Maj. Gen. Harding (as he then was), Field Marshal Alexander's* Chief of Staff, in the battle for Rome (which mercifully became an open city).

The 1st Marine Division could look back with pride on its achievement which had brought it within rifle range of Seoul itself. But now it was not Puller or Murray or even Barr over the Han, but both divisions under the overall command of X Corps; and Kim Il-sung was not going to make it easy for Almond. The Corps commander was in a hurry to cross the river, as Smith recorded while emphasizing the disadvantages:

> It will be necessary for the 7th Division to take over its zone of action south of us. So far, Puller has been forced to protect his own south flank. . . . Then it is necessary for the 5th Marines in the area facing Yongdungpo in order that the 5th Marines can assemble its battalions for the crossing. Then there is the question of bridging material. . . . General Almond

* Alexander was the Supreme Commander in Italy.

promises bridging material. This is an empty promise, as the 1st Marine Division has the only bridging material available.[5]

If the Marines knew that they alone possessed this material since Lt. Col. H. Partridge, commander of the 1st Marine Engineer Battalion, who had been aware of his unit's monopoly since he had, with foresight, stocked its resources at San Diego, how could such a misunderstanding honestly have occurred? Once again, one is bound to detect a certain gloating by the Marines, right up to their 1st Divisional Commander himself, over the Army's deficiency, which did not induce strong allegiance at a time when it was needed. Either MacArthur was kept in ignorance of all this, or he felt that Almond's plans were going ahead without a hitch. MacArthur was, after all, the supreme strategist who delegated the tactics to others.

Smith ordered the 5th Marines to cross the Han at Haenju on D+5, seize Hill 125, turn southeast up the right bank and uncover crossing sites for the 1st Marines. The tactics would be Murray's. They were bold. Capt. Houghton, two naval officers, two Army officers and nine other ranks would swim the river after dark and reconnoiter the far bank and the lower slopes of Hill 125, the ominous shape that dominated the eastern approach. The crossing site, in fact, would be contained within a triangle of the hills, 125, 95, and 51. Taplett's 3/5th Marines and a column of 2/1st Marines would then cross through Houghton's company screen and wheel towards Seoul, using amtracs. All went according to plan and the swimmers radioed their successful crossing as a prelude to the rest of Houghton's men's occupation of high ground a mile away, while the rest of the 5th Marines just hoped for the best. But Murray had failed to take account of the enemy's possible moves and no sooner were the swimmers zeroing their positions than Hill 125 erupted and caught the amtracs in mid-stream. Houghton was badly shocked by a blast and several casualties were sustained. The Marines withdrew to the west bank, bringing their casualties with them. They had withdrawn a second time, but it would be the last. With the world's press looking over Murray's shoulder while he issued his orders, it was a severe embarrassment.

The crossing now fell to Taplett's 3/5th Marines, the heroes of Wolmi-do. H-Hour would be 0645 and the men would be transported by LTV's in waves of six craft. The companies would move across in column, I to H, until the river bank was secured, the offending Hill 125 taken and the country seized back to Hill 51, beyond the Kaesong-Seoul railway. The Marines pressed ahead with their daunting task, suffering relatively heavy casualties from communist firepower on Hill 125 which had such a commanding view of the Americans. The weapons company, particularly, was heavily hit and it was only with the greatest courage and tenacity that the Marines' sparse machine gun fire could be maintained to cover the assaulting troops. The raking fire of four Corsairs had done little to quell the NKPA's enthusiasm for what their propaganda leaflets during the war described as military power which "would wound their families with arrows of keen pang."[6]* But Taplett did not have to fight so intensely for every inch to Hill 51. The NKPA in front of McMullen's company suddenly got up and left. Over 200 of their comrades lay dead, while the Marines suffered 43 dead and wounded. But here the enemy was cracked wide open. At 1000 hours Roise crossed the Han with his 2nd Battalion and consolidated the positions which Taplett's battalion had won. He was followed by the 2nd Battalion, Korean Marines, which had already spread out northward to occupy the Kumpo Peninsula, the land mass pointing north by northwest at Inchon.

Murray's progress on D+6 was henceforth calm and without much incident; but the enemy was busy reinforcing the 78th Regiment's depleted garrison which had fallen back on Seoul with five thousand communists, commanded by the Russian-trained Maj. Gen. Wol Ki-chan. This will be referred to again in the next chapter, for indeed Gen. Wol's stand on the northwestern outskirts of Seoul was the most determined resistance which the US forces were to encounter throughout *Chromite*.

When Almond assumed formal command ashore on the evening of D+6, the Han had been crossed; and all objectives surrounding Seoul, except those from the east, had been taken. The new 7th Marines were placed on the extreme left (northern) flank, ready to cut off the enemy fleeing from the projected thrust of the 5th Marines. In the south the 7th Division was

---

* I am indebted to Col. Robert Debs Heinl, Jr., for this information.

consolidating its position and the cutting of the road to Anyang effectively prevented the enemy from being reinforced on this flank as it had been by Gen. Wol's horde in the north. This was the major menace, and since Almond had decreed that the capture of Seoul was to be an entirely Marine affair,* with the 7th Division's boundary running along the Han, Smith felt that he could move Puller's Regiment into line with Murray's in order to hold what might be the best part of 10,000 NKPA on the northwestern sector of the city.

This surprise reinforcement of the enemy's forces did not deter Almond's intention to capture Seoul by D+10, September 25th. He was impatient with the Marines' progress and threatened to alter the boundaries in X Corps, a suggestion which was understandably opposed by Smith who did not wish to injure his division's tactical integrity. Almond suggested that the 5th Marines should be halted northwest of Seoul and the 1st Marines, instead of supporting the 5th Regiment from the northwest by west be brought around to attack from the southeast. Smith urged that the 1st Marines should attack from Yongdungpo, across the Han, and the 7th be allowed to approach from the north. It had already been arranged that in order to protect the left flank of the Division in the Kumpo Peninsula (often mistakenly called Kimpo, which name applies only to the village near which the airfield was sited) the 187th Airborne R.C.T. should be flown out from Japan to strengthen the K.M.C. Regiment. Relenting, Almond decided instead to send the 32nd Regiment and the R.O.K. 17th Regiment of the 7th Division into the center of Seoul from the southeast by a wide sweeping movement which would seal off all southern approaches and so cross the Han due south of the city. This they achieved on September 25th in Marine amtracs and advanced swiftly towards South Mountain which dominated the capital.

Almond did not achieve his impossible target of capturing Seoul by D+10 (90 days after the Korean invasion); instead, on that date, X Corps was merely poised to move in on its final objective.

---

* The Corps commander, as we will see, was later to have reservations about this.

CHAPTER NINE

Seoul and Euphoria

The battle for Seoul is difficult to define precisely. Essentially, the action occurred between September 19–20th and September 28th, 1950. On September 20th, Gen. Shepherd confided in his diary, "I personally believe it will take a week of fighting before Seoul is secured." While Col. Heinl prefers to include the fighting with Gen. Wol's men northwest of the capital as part of a separate chapter devoted to the crossing of the Han, I feel that the struggle for Seoul itself began when the 5th Marines crossed the Han as early as D+5. The ridges used by Wol on the city's northwestern and northern flanks, in the latter case where there is no river, were tactically strong places from which fire could be sent southward on the 1st Marines as they approached Seoul from Yongdungpo, the Han, and the inner suburb of Sogang, and northwest as they struck at Taplett's 3/5th Marines who had already crossed the Han well downstream, opposite Kumpo.

The Russian-trained Gen. Wol,* whose presence was a sinister foreboding of alien help and a bonanza for the North Koreans, nevertheless could not hope to halt the drive on Seoul while the Americans were allowed to keep supremacy in the air. At best he could try only to stem the link up between MacArthur and Walker and prevent as many NKPA as possible from being caught in the pocket which the U.N. was about to create. It

* So *Wolmi-do* means Little Moon-tip Island and *Wol* is Korean for *Moon*. The *Wols* of North Korea have usually remained with that name, while in South Korea many have anglicized their names, such as Mr. Moon, the evangelist.

was too late to drive the invaders back into the sea at Inchon. Had that been the communists' intention it should have been implemented days before. No, this was simply a holding action in which the enemy threw in everything it had but the majority of its supplies were being directed to the wrong front.

The high ground held by Gen. Wol was Hill 296, a massif known locally as An-San, which was a bare feature (now overgrown with a sprawling suburb, rendering it almost unrecognizable) from which protruded several spurs. The 78th Independent Regiment, the defenders of Seoul, had under command 2,000 infantry with reinforcements of light artillery, engineers, and heavy weapons commanded by Colonel Pal Han-lin, whose first task was to delay Murray's assault across the Han from Kumpo. We have already seen from Houghton's and Taplett's points of view the unexpected success the Colonel had.

Early on D+7, the morning after Almond had assumed command of X Corps ashore, Murray placed three battalions in line. Taplett's 3rd Battalion was on the left (northern) flank where, from Hill 216, he was poised to take An-San beyond the steep valley of Sachon Creek. He was then to hold 296 as a pivot, with his battalions arranged in companies from left to right, over the ridges to Seoul. It was a severe task. In the center Murray placed the Korean Marines who were to attack across a deep valley, capture a ridge ahead of them (Hill 56), and continue to take two farther hills, both called 105. The 1st battalion on the right was to engage Hill 68 and attack another called 105. These were duly called 105 North, Central, and South, only three of the spurs radiating outward from An-San. The only confusing result of naming hills after their height is when the theodolite is too accurate.

Despite a hot reception Taplett achieved his mission with remarkable success. Having so repeatedly commanded the 5th Marines' reserve battalion he showed fine qualities of leadership here as in the crossing of the Han and, indeed, when his own and Maj. Kim's Marines had been surprised by the enemy in Ascom City. The South Korean Marines had the hottest reception of all on D+7, but were heavily supported from the air. That day VMF-323 flew 42 sorties, only one less than the record flown by any VMF on D-Day. But from the right, Newton's battalion was ordered by Murray to bypass the ridge which lay between 105S and 296, itself divided from the dominating northern feature, 338, only by the Seoul–Kaesong road.

Newton attacked 105 South with heavy losses among his officers, including a casualty sustained when a bullet passed between a man's esophagus and his spinal column without grazing either, an operation hard enough with a scalpel from within three inches, let alone from a chance shot by a bullet at a hundred yards. Many acts of gallantry were performed at this stage. Finally, before dusk, the companies of Capts. Pederson and Fenton took 105 South by storm. Meanwhile, well over to the east, the NKPA was fleeing northward with the Eighth Army imminently on its tail. Overall, Newton's and Taplett's men were up, but the South Korean Marines were back where they had started.

Next morning opened with a fierce grenade and mortar fight on the eastern slopes of Hill 105 South, before it was finally won by the Marines. Murray then pulled in his reserve battalion under Roise to help the K.M.C. capture Hill 56. Marine losses were heavier at this than at any other stage of *Chromite*. Companies D, E, and F skillfully employed fire and movement and wasted no opportunity to move fast at every opportunity; they also made the most of a railway tunnel and a sunken road to vanish and reappear in order to win their objective. As night fell on September 23rd the Marines were pinned down in their foxholes, and the country was such that General Wol's troops were quite equal to Almond's firepower.

It was at this uneasy stage, when Almond was becoming impatient of Marine progress, that the X Corps commander considered reorganizing his attack on central Seoul by dividing the Marines and, to Smith's chagrin, strengthening the northwestern approaches by a stiffening of army units. This suggestion did not go down at all well and, erring on the side of discretion, as we have seen, Almond dropped his ideas. We know of his ultimate plan, but behind his impatience to capture Seoul by September 25th, one is bound to see the urgent figure of MacArthur himself, perhaps with justifiable pride, waiting anxiously for the chance to hand power back to Syngman Rhee in the battle-scarred Capitol Building in Seoul. Here is depicted the unfortunate Almond, divided in his loyalties as Commander of X Corps and Chief of Staff to Gen. MacArthur.

The northwestern defense was broken by a series of out-flanking movements. But what Smith regarded as a far more significant nicety than anything diplomatic occurred when the 1st and 5th Marines joined up in the city beyond. The enemy withdrew northward into the hills. Only Smith had watched the 1st Marines under the redoubtable Colonel Puller cross the Han from Yongdungpo on September 24th, while on the southern flank there was a large crowd of star-studded spectators. But now it was the army's turn for the limelight.

The indigenous 31st R.O.K. (Seoul) Regiment was anxious to strike out to Hill 348, the great southern prominence of the city, and be the first to see their capital's panorama again, and not even Almond would try to stop them. Then there was also an American marine, the scion of three generations of missionaries in Korea, who learned that the former mission station in which he had been born and brought up was now in enemy hands as one of Wol's command posts, if not his headquarters. Without hesitation he passed the information back to his battalion commander who called up the marine artillery. Within a minute the work and devotion of this young officer's family and forebears would, so far as its tangible value is concerned, completely vanish in a heap of dust.

Seoul was described in the official history as a "flak trap." Certainly air losses among the Americans were heavy on September 23-24th, and several distinguished pilots were killed, including Maj. Floeck and Lt. Col. Lischeid. But heavy though these were, this was the last severe enemy resistance to *Operation Chromite*.

Over the rivers and their tributaries the Marines and soldiers became urban snipers from rooftops, down alleyways, and at road junctions. Every man became his own Al Capone or Sitting Bull (Custer's old 7th Cavalry was making its way up from Pusan). Then the Commander in Chief became his own Alexander the Great, amid what the British journalist and author of *Cry Korea*, R. W. Thompson, called "so terrible a liberation." He formally handed back the presidency of South Korea to Syngman Rhee in an emotional ceremony in the

Capitol two days after the enemy was supposed to have surrendered Seoul, but not before the last of them reappeared, as
they had done at Ascom City, from the town drains.

MacArthur had restored authority over the Philippines to
Osmena in February, 1945, had accepted the Japanese surrender on the USS *Missouri* in Tokyo Bay and had even restored authority to the deputy mayor of Inchon. Clearly, he
enjoyed this kind of pageantry in which the military powers
seem to have been deliverers of civil authority. When shown
over the *Missouri* in Inchon only a few days earlier his tears of
nostalgia were quite evident and his nature transparent. He
had wept as unquestionably as Churchill when the Prime Minister was taken to see the effect of the Blitz on the East End.
MacArthur had no feeling that he should restrain himself, as
those to whom weeping is alien and, except in certain allow-
able cases, definitely undignified. Why should MacArthur or
Churchill care about the consensus of opinion? They were both
prone to catharsis and were incurable romantics long after ro-
mance and war had parted company in the bushveld of South
Africa. Despite his British name, MacArthur was in many ways
more reminiscent of Napoleon than Wellington. Ethnically he
was to Britain what the Macedonian, Alexander the Great, was
to Greece.

As for the Seoul that re-emerged as a free city after the
euphoria and the speeches (not suspecting another brief period
of communist occupation early in 1951), let us think not of
MacArthur, the U.S. Marine Corps, Kim Il-sung, or Wol, but
simply of the young South Korean violinist, Kyong Wha-chung,
who is known throughout the musical world as a prodigious
exponent of Beethoven, Mendelssohn, and, with her sister, of
Brahms' Double Concerto. When the Marines crossed the Han
she was yet unborn. It is no banality to ponder on the phenomenon that had Douglas MacArthur not conceived the idea
of *Operation Chromite* Kyong Wha-chung would probably
never have had the opportunity to develop her gifts, if indeed
she had existed at all. I simply wish to indicate a curious
situation rather than pose an unanswerable question of the kind
which would have preoccupied Thornton Wilder and Martin
Heidegger.

The criterion of a great soldier, beside a complete mastery of his skill, is that ultimately he propagates the civilization for which von Clausewitz's politicians strove in vain. Alexander the Great propagated the teachings of his own tutor, Aristotle, and Napoleon (albeit the ultimate military loser) redefined a law and a purpose for France. Alexander died at 33, Napoleon's military career ended when he was 46 and MacArthur's at 70. His most outstanding work, of course, was in the Pacific; his methods were so unorthodox that his legacy, at this close proximity, is still elusive. But I feel sure that the sublime virtuosity of Kyong Wha-chung, the life he unwittingly created, would have brought him to a state of catharsis and made more pronounced his patriotic fervor and personal repute as the restorer of order and cultured progress.

CHAPTER TEN

The Link-up

The initial problem facing MacArthur, as the objectives of *Chromite* were about to be achieved, was to arouse the Eighth Army from its inertia in the Pusan Perimeter where the disparity of rival forces has already been mentioned. From time to time it seemed that Walker's dispirited men were making efforts to release themselves from their habitual bondage, but it was difficult at a distance to distinguish between the beginning of an offensive or a counter-attack merely to prevent closer communist approach. Nor was it easy to know when the rear of the encircling army was beginning to move northward as the prelude to a retreat. Walker, however, had first attempted to break out on September 16th (D+1), and by September 19th he was across the Naktong in force.

By September 23rd, however, when X Corps was hammering on the doors of Seoul, the first enemy retreat from the perimeter could be discerned. They could see that unless they moved while there was still time they would be hopelessly trapped. MacArthur and Kim Il-sung now both foresaw the threat of the hammer on the anvil as an immediate reality.

But speed was X Corps' priority, and Walker was told that he must make contact with the beachhead, however slight. On September 23rd the 1st Cavalry Division, taking advantage of the NKPA's increasing weakness in the perimeter, was ordered to break out and push up the central corridor, along the road between Taegu (which had been Walker's headquarters throughout the siege) and Osan. The Divisional Commander, Maj.

Gen. Hobart R. Gay, delegated this task to the 3/7th Cavalry under Lt. Col. James H. Lynch who, as "Task Force Lynch," became the spearhead of the breakout. By September 26th, they had little more than a hundred miles to go, driving what, under normal circumstances, would be a perilously attenuated advance into enemy country. But Lynch knew that he was safe because as he raced northward he passed bedraggled NKPA soldiers retreating in a fruitless effort to escape strangulation and cheering South Koreans who could afford to feel delighted although their homes were in ruins. Three Pershings accompanied Lynch, but they moved so fast that radio contact was eventually lost. For its part the 7th Infantry Division had advanced southward from Suwon to Osan, a mere ten miles distant, and were there to greet the Pershings when, at 2000 hours on September 26th, the tanks reached Osan. The hands were grasped at last. This was a moment of real euphoria, but contact was dangerously tenuous until, at 0826 hours next day, L Troop of the 7th Cavalry closed up and strengthened the delicate liaison.

Many hundreds of North Koreans changed into civilian clothes and evaporated into the hills, but of the 70,000 who had held Walker around Pusan it is estimated that only 25,000 managed to recross the 38th parallel. The 2nd NKPA Division, for example, now possessed only 200 officers and men. The Eighth Army took 9,294 prisoners and destroyed or captured 239 T-34 tanks and 74 76-mm self-propelled guns. All these losses, together with those unaccounted for, are in addition to the casualties and captured booty estimated by X Corps and examined in figures mentioned at the beginning of the next chapter.

MacArthur himself had "never shone more brightly" than at this moment. Bearing in mind even World War II, this, because of the reputation he had already established and upon which any further victories must be an embellishment, was the highest moment of his military career. One may talk the subject into wild exaggeration but here was what is made to sound like a banality, the moment of truth, in the life of one man, and some of those who wrote or spoke in his name might have been happier if it had ended there. But the current thought was that

The Link-Up

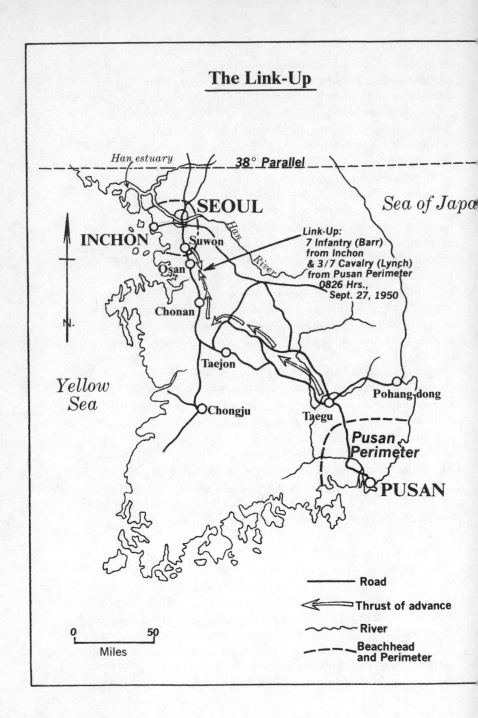

Han estuary

38° Parallel

SEOUL

Sea of Japa

INCHÒN

Suwon

Han River

Link-Up:
7 Infantry (Barr)
from Inchon
& 3/7 Cavalry (Lynch)
from Pusan Perimeter
0826 Hrs.,
Sept. 27, 1950

Osan

N.

Chonan

Taejon

Yellow
Sea

Chongju

Taegu

Pohang-dong

Pusan
Perimeter

PUSAN

Road

Thrust of advance

River

Beachhead
and Perimeter

0   50

Miles

if MacArthur could execute *Operation Chromite*, he could do anything. Even before it was finished he was looking ahead to that unachieved landing at Wonsan. But, as events turned out, the speed with which the released Eighth Army moved up the east coast completely precluded it.

Now came the pursuit of the retreating NKPA. At this stage the 7th Marines played a vital part in capturing Uijongbu, which is an important road and railway junction at the north of a long defile from Seoul. It is also at the western end of long road and railway lines from Wonsan, which is Korea's major east coast port. It fell to the 2nd Battalion under Maj. William D. Sawyer of Litzenenberg's 11th Regiment to undertake this operation at 1700 hours on October 3rd. To witness the final stage of *Chromite* was Gen. Cates, now the ecstatic Commandant of the Marine Corps, and Maj. Gen. Frank Lowe, the huge, bony 60-year-old representative in Korea of President Truman, whose presence was unnerving both for this apparently furtive reason and because he and Cates delighted in the insecurity of being where the fighting was. Cates, evidently unaware of the concern which he himself was causing in this respect, was critical of Lowe for creating undue anxiety. Col. Heinl's book, however, includes a photograph of the Marine Corps Commandant in a front line trench north of Seoul.

On the day Seoul officially fell (September 28th) X Corps eventually brought up their own bridging equipment which would be needed for MacArthur's triumphal entry. The climax of the operation, as mentioned, was MacArthur's own device, the formal handing back of power over South Korea to Dr. Syngman Rhee in the battle-scarred Capitol Building in Seoul. No commander in modern times had found humility equal to Allenby's entry into Damascus, striding in on foot and leading his white charger by its reins, a gesture which so impressed his spectators, but MacArthur's practice was impressive enough and more in keeping with the indigenous Koreans. Nevertheless he was criticized by the Pentagon for taking this authority on himself, but it made him a great hero and gave the people a self-respect they badly needed. Washington's motives were entirely political, for to obviate unnecessary embarrassment (and clearly Syngman was an intransigent ally) they wanted as little to do with him as with Chiang Kai-shek. But if Syngman was criticized for his mode of leadership and alleged barbarity, the United Nations had only to witness the barbarity that lay in the wake of the retreating communists to gain a sense of Korean proportion. Everywhere the U.N. forces found heaps, each of several thousand bodies, buried in shallow graves. In Taejon alone the U.N. troops found the bodies of between 5,000 and 7,000 South Korean civilians.

X Corps was not given to Walker, but, as I mentioned in the first chapter, was maintained under the command of Gen. Almond under the personal supervision of MacArthur. If such strategy as the Inchon landing was evidently so successful then there was no knowing what X Corps could achieve in North Korea.

Strategically, *Operation Chromite* ended with the capture of Seoul and the link-up between the X Corps and the Eighth Army. But MacArthur was *Chromite* personified, and while he was grievously disappointed by the subsequent retreat of the U.N. forces before the Chinese invasion, his Inchon attitude to war, of the cut and thrust cavalier, did not leave the Far East until he was recalled home by his President whom he had met only once.

CHAPTER ELEVEN

The Cost

The American casualties in *Operation Chromite* were as follows:

	Fatal casualties	Wounded	Missing	Total
U.S. Marine Corps (Incl. U.S. Marine Air Wing).	422	2,031	6	2,459
U.S. Army	106	411	57	574
U.S. Navy	8	118	2	128
	536	2,560	65	3,161

No definitive breakdown of ROK military casualties was ever made during the Korean War because of the difficulties of identifying the corpses as from the north or south (when not even uniform was a reliable identification), and between soldier and civilian. But, by way of comparison, while the United States lost nearly 34,000 dead throughout the entire war the approximate South Korean losses were 47,000. The only other allied casualties throughout the whole of *Chromite* were sustained on board HMS *Jamaica* where one sailor was killed and two wounded. Enemy casualties figures are inevitably more inaccurate. X Corps estimated that the NKPA lost 14,000 killed and 7,000 wounded which are curious relative totals.

Concerning allied and enemy arms, the figures seem to be remarkably accurate. About 50 T-34 tanks were destroyed, of which the Marines claimed 47 by ground or air attack. The Marines also claimed to have destroyed or captured 23 120 mm mortars (a particularly notorious Russian weapon), two 76 mm self-propelled guns, eight 76 mm conventional guns, 19 45 mm anti-tank guns, 59 14.5 mm anti-tank rifles, 56 heavy machine guns and 7,543 rifles. The amount of reclaimed American weapons has never been quantified, but was considerable. The X Corps Tactical Air Command flew 2,533 sorties during the operation at the cost of 11 American aircraft, all destroyed by enemy groundfire. Communist aerial cover was negligible and did not become threatening until the use of Mig-15s during their counterattack in the spring of 1951. The U.S. Marine Air Wing dropped 5,328 bombs and 50,420 pounds of napalm. 5,269 naval shells and rockets of 6-in. caliber or heavier (including British) were fired, as were 7,117 5-in. shells, 14,526 rockets (mostly 5-in.), 519 3-in. shells and 860,047 40-mm, 20-mm, and .50-caliber projectiles, the last-named mostly from aircraft.

Perhaps it should be recorded that the Korean War witnessed two innovations; first, the free mixture in platoons and sections of white and black U.S. soldiers and marines; and second, for the first time, the use on active service of helicopters which were invaluable, particularly as direct communication between Army headquarters and M*A*S*H units.

The most contentious issue which troubled the commanders at Inchon (with the notable exception of MacArthur) was the X Corps command structure which, as I have already mentioned, gave MacArthur's able Chief of Staff the additional responsibility of command over X Corps. Even to have promoted him to the appropriate corps commander rank of lieutenant general would have helped to strengthen his authority. But since most of the fighting was undertaken by the 1st Marine Division it could understandably be argued that the Corps should have been commanded by Maj. Gen. Smith; or, detached exclusively for this operation alone, by the Marine general of corps commander rank, Lt. Gen. Shepherd. But, of course, Almond alone was privy to MacArthur's earliest plans and of the Commander in Chief's later intention of using X Corps on the east coast. In an essentially amphibious operation, however, it was argued by the Marines that an Army general would be unfamiliar with proper landing procedure, a disadvantage which would be further vitiated by the speed with which *Chromite* had to be planned. But, in the event, the landing was substantially a Marine affair, Almond not taking command until he came ashore on D+6. That the landing was so successful was remarkable; but, quite apart from X Corps command, several errors occurred which were the result of little or no adequate rehearsal. For this, no one can be blamed; it was the essential hazard of the operation.

Korea has tended to become a forgotten war. For some curious reason the British, albeit represented by two brigades in the field, think more of the less costly conflicts, such as Malaya, Aden, and even Suez, before considering the drastic consequences which could have resulted from a mismanagement of the allied offensive or weakness at the negotiating tables at Kaesong or Panmunjom. For the citizen of the United States, Korea is still only marginally less taboo than Vietnam, though a whole generation has grown to manhood since the Korean War ended. Without stirring unhappy memories too acutely, we have come to accept the television program, M*A*S*H, while a comedy set in Vietnam would be out of the question for Americans. Perhaps, so far as the British are concerned, an undercurrent of jealousy of the United States' military superiority since World War II and a reversal of the *status quo*, have precluded an acknowledgment of the brilliance of *Operation Chromite*, considered apart from its disastrous aftermath (I will not say "consequence"), and robbed it of the acclaim it deserves. But this was never evident in Korea itself. Certainly, while the United States had inevitably become a military superpower, the British had no cause to feel ashamed of their contribution to the United Nations' cause. They had shown bravery second to none. When David Rees wrote of a "Twentieth Century Cannae" he spoke in Britain for a small proportion of those who are remotely interested and represented the few who would even have remembered what he was talking about.

The loss of Korea would have been disastrous. Inchon saved it.

I believe that inter-service rivalry in the United States also detracted from *Chromite*'s success; while, making the same point, Col. Heinl quoted Gen. Smith's laconic remark that the failure of the U.S. Army to award its Distinguished Service Citation to the First Marine Division was "not accidental." [1]

MacArthur's last and most outstanding triumph was sandwiched between two disasters which seem to be far more readily recalled to the public mind. Ironically, they were the one which *Chromite* overcame and the other which, some argue, *Chromite* created. But that the General may have been unwise to pursue the North Koreans to the Manchurian frontier (militarily justifiable, but politically and diplomatically fatal) must be regarded as a separate issue. *Operation Chromite* was a short and definable operation which achieved its aim against all prediction within a mere fortnight. This book has sought only to describe the way MacArthur implemented the Inchon landings, pursuing them to the capture of Seoul and the break-out of the Eighth Army, and reminds readers that however unwise MacArthur may have been to enter North Korea or drive to the Yalu he did not start the war. Faced with the wholly unjustifiable aggression which the enemy showed on June 24, 1950, he applied a strategist's answer and has been blamed for the consequences ever since by friend and foe alike. The first chapter of this book gives a brief, but impartial, history of the events leading up to the communist hostilities in 1950. That *Pravda*, the mouthpiece of the Russian Government, should have declared on September 23rd that "the situation is very serious" [2] emphasizes the United Nations' military success at Inchon which became a justifiable spearhead of a second front to save an entrapped army.

The Korean War revitalized the United States' armed forces and put them back on a healthier conventional footing at a time when several sinister methods of waging a successful war, even apart from the atom bomb, were being considered in an attempt to achieve swift victory and reduce military manpower. One advantage of having an outstanding (if headstrong) commander to conduct operations, albeit with set ideas as to what constitutes victory and defeat, is that he is peculiarly able to correct the imbalance between conventional warfare and the race towards newer and swifter means of human destruction. It is a paradox of MacArthur that this should be so, while he is still regarded in the popular mind as the warmonger who brought the world to the edge of atomic war. Inchon illustrated that only advanced conventional weapons were suitable in this, the war that changed war. But, as I have emphasized, MacArthur was more than just an ageing conservative commander. His attributes need not be reiterated, except to repeat that his "reckless and defiant insolence" alone refused to accept defeat and, with Churchillian imagination, he conceived of a means of giving the enemy a thrashing from which, despite his own subsequent setback, they never really recovered, as any comparison of the situations on June 24, 1950, with July 27, 1953, will support. But for diplomatic restraint, rather than military inadequacy, there is no doubt in this author's mind that the United Nations would have been seen to conclude the war with greater military success. But such views are unfashionable these days while the world watches the illusion of disarmament. Walker, I repeat, was losing a thousand casualties a day in the Pusan perimeter while MacArthur was imploring the Joint Chiefs of Staff to be allowed to attack Inchon. Had he not had his way, it is difficult to see how he could have saved Korea and then the offshore islands. The opposition in the Pentagon to the conception of *Bluehearts* and *Chromite* (the former having given them advance warning of the Commander in Chief's true eccentricity) makes us bound to believe that only MacArthur could have done it. But had Korea been surrendered the danger in Europe would have been no less acute.

At Green Beach on Wolmi-do Island there stands a small cenotaph, inaccurately attributing the landing to the 7th Infantry Division (which must cause the Marines some irritation). But nevertheless the South Koreans, who would not be expected to distinguish between the various arms of the American and South Korean fighting services, pay punctilious homage to their deliverers each year. Perhaps, while this candle of memory is kept alight in an otherwise indifferent world, history will eventually decide upon the achievements of the Inchon landings. It is not simple to appraise the subject in the immediate aftermath of a style of war, albeit a quarter of a century dead, which vanished overnight and of which Korea spelt the epilogue. War, according to the old school, was waged to win victory in the wake of total political and diplomatic breakdown and establish a new peace, the fruits of which would be a fresh opportunity to strive for the vaguely conceived notions of progress and happiness, even though they are the fruits of the victor's aggrandizement. But the price of war has become immeasurably sinister, so that peace assumes terrible proportions of its own. Certainly, war is less easily definable today, and has changed totally since the 3/5th Marines stormed Wolmi-do. So has peace. The most limited of all wars, so science has determined, is the explosion of a neutron bomb.

The Diary of
Operation Chromite

D-Day: September 15, 1950
H-Hour: Green Beach, 0630 hours;
Red and Blue Beaches, 1730 hours

I: PRE-INVASION

D-Day—14: Lt. Eugene Clark, USN, and a small party are put ashore (Operation *Trudy Jackson*), following such a landing by Lt. Lee (Korean Marine Corps) on August 19th, to carry out a thorough reconnaissance of Inchon (height of seawall, nature of mudflats, tides, defenses, etc., duly signalled to the USS *Mount McKinley*). Results prove vitally important. Clark awarded Navy Cross.

D-Day—10
and 11: Ships of the Royal Navy (Rear Adm. W. Andrewes, RN), shell Wolmi-do from northern approaches in order to confuse the enemy as to the U.N.'s direction of approach; if, indeed, the enemy believes Inchon to be the target of the anticipated invasion.

D—5: Beginning of intense softening-up operations.

Night of
D—2 and 3 To confuse the enemy, Kunsan is assaulted by a force from the frigate, HMS *Whitesand Bay*, consisting of U.S. Special Operations Coy (Col. Louis B. Ely) and a unit of 41 Marine Commando (Lt.

E. G. D. Pounds); three U.S. fatalities. The same
force tries to grab Kimpo on D+1 and 2.

D—2:   USS *Mount McKinley* (Doyle's flagship), with
MacArthur and his entire staff (rather unwisely *in
toto*) aboard, preceded by the Support Group, casts
off from Sasebo, Japan.

D—2:   All escort carriers in the area of Inchon.

D—2:   Cruisers and destroyers nose their way into Flying
Fish Channel from the south, just north of Yonghungdo (Yonghung Island). Mines already encountered.

D—2,
1242 hours: USS *Gurke* drops anchor 3 miles north of Wolmi-
do.

D—2,
1255 hours: Battle commences.

D—2,
1347 hours: Cdor. Allen orders planned retirement of destroyers after the initial bombardment.

D—1,
1116 hours: The cruisers (HMS *Jamaica* and *Kenya* and USS
Rochester and *Toledo*) open fire at Blue and Red
Beaches with 6- and 8-in. guns.

Midnight,
D—1, and
D-Day: The fleet re-forms station at entrance to Flying
Fish Channel.

II: INVASION

Green Beach

D-Day,
0254 hours: Destroyers of 90.1 hem the target area.

0454 hours: First aircraft orbit the invasion beach.

0520 hours: Signal from the yardarm of the *Mount McKinley,* "Land the Landing Force."

0545 hours: Cruisers open fire.

0600 hours: Landing force takes to the boats.

0600–
0615 hours: Marine Corsairs give the target area a final solo aerial assault.

0633 hours
(3 minutes
late):   3/5 Marines (Lt. Col. Taplett) land on Wolmi-do.

D-Day,
0659 hours: Capt. McMullen's I Coy advances through North Point in the wake of H Coy, when they are met by grenade-throwing NKPA of about one platoon strength. Enemy ignore orders to surrender, so most of them are sealed into their bunkers by Pershings and tank-dozers. A few, numbed and bleeding, do surrender in time. This is a brutal and very questionable expedient which may well be contrary to the rules of war.

Before
0730 hours: Half the island is occupied.

0745 hours: Lt. Col. Taplett (commanding 3/5 Marines) reports light resistance to Gen. Smith on *Mount McKinley,* and 105-meter Radio Hill is almost entirely in Lt. Bohn's hands.

0800 hours: Radio Hill occupied, as is the whole island except So Wolmi-do at the southern end of Green Beach; but this is sternly defended.

1048 hours: The end of the causeway is occupied after a napalm attack.

1115 hours: Main fighting on Green Beach concluded.

1215 hours: Green Beach fully controlled after final mopping-up.

Red Beach

D-Day,
noon: Rear Adm. Higgins' Support Group (4 cruisers and 6 destroyers) begins the final bombardment; Rear Adm. Ewen's Fast Carriers defend the ships by sealing off the invasion area with use of heavy AD's (500- and 1000-pound bombs) which disrupt all enemy movement within 25 miles of Inchon. USS *Boxer* reinforces Corsair squadrons.

D-Day,
1430 hours: USS *Toledo* and *Rochester,* using spotter aircraft, hit the eastern and north-eastern sectors of Inchon with 260-pound, 8-in. shells.

D-Day,
1550 onwards: All aircraft (above) bomb the target area. Task Force 77 keeps 12 aircraft continuously aloft by rotation (also over Green and Blue Beaches).

D-Day,
1704 hours: LCVP's, with leading companies, riding off-shore.

1724 hours: Signal given: the following first 8 LCVP's race towards northern Inchon:
2 pns A Coy 1 Bn and E Coy 2Bn 5 Marines, with 3/5 Marines' heavy supporting weapons.

1733 hours: 3 of the 4 leading LCVP's strike the seawall; southern Red Beach assaulted.

1733 hours: On the most northerly beach of Red the rest reach the shore, except one break-down.
Heavy casualties and fire fight before break-out from all parts of Red; fighting especially severe in

the northern sector; here Lt. Baldomero Lopez wins the first Medal of Honor at Inchon.

1775 hours: Cemetery Hill completely captured.

1800 hours: Eight aged LST's waddle ashore to draw the enemy's fire and spot his defenses; of marginal value.

1830 hours: Lt. Col. Murray (commander 5 Marines) lands at Red Beach.

2300 hours: Reconnaissance into Inchon.

2359 hours: Red Beach designated area completely cleared of enemy and Observatory Hill finally secured.

Blue Beach

D-Day,
1400 hours: First LCVP's move early to command boats because of heavy swell and speed of the current (3½ knots).

1430 hours: HMS *Jamaica* and *Kenya* (6-in. shells) begin bombardment of Blue Beach—the former concentrating on Tok Am, the southern promontory.

1645 hours: Eighteen LVT(A)'s, with the first wave of 1 Marines, cross the line of departure and set off on a 5,500-yard approach to Blue Beach.

D-Day,
1730 hours: The first three waves reach their allotted destinations.

1800 hours: All battalions and their respective assault companies ashore. An extra beach, adjacent, is discovered (Blue 2 and Yellow).

2000 hours: D Coy captures road junction (Able).

2200 hours: F Coy is entrenched on Hill 117 (Dog).

D-Day+1,
0130 hours: Col. Puller reports to Gen. Smith that Blue Beach
               is completely secured.

By D-Day+2:   All 1 Marine Division armor ashore at Inchon
               (via Blue 2).

III: BREAKOUT TO SEOUL

D-Day+1,
0500 hours: Corsairs knock-out 6 T-34 tanks beyond the
               coastal ridges.

0650 hours: Two more tanks knocked-out and infantry rein-
               forcements for Inchon straffed; heavy enemy
               casualties.

1600 hours: Puller reaches 0-3 Line; Sutter's battalion has a
               tough fight to gain ground.

About dusk: Gen. Smith's beachhead is secured; while 5 Ma-
               rines overlook Ascom City and so command the
               Forward Beachhead Line; but Puller is a mile
               behind. He secures the exposed southern flank
               at the point where the beachhead regains the
               coast.

Night,
D+1 to 2:   South Korean Marines (Lt. Col. Shin Hyun-jun)
               "mop-up" beachhead.

D+1 and
   D+2:   Enemy advance in strength to reconnaissance
               from Yongdungpo, Ascom City and westward.
               Murray, with aerial warning, lays a pocket of fire-
               power and causes heavy casualties on the NKPA
               infantry.

D+2,
first light: Two enemy aircraft attempt to bomb and strafe USS *Rochester* and HMS *Jamaica* at Inchon; one British sailor killed.

D+2,
0700 hours: South Korean Marine Coy from 5 Marine begins breakout northwards.

D+2, early: Gen. Smith resumes command of Marine Division ashore. His H.Q. is established on Yellow Beach.

D-Day+2:   Almost immediately Gen. MacArthur and his staff come ashore to inspect the positions, present awards for gallantry and visit the men. Welcomed on Yellow Beach by Gen. Smith.

D+2,
0700 to
1000 hours: 1 Marines launch break-out from Blue Beach, led by 2 Bn (Sutter). Stiff resistance encountered, especially in the northern sector of the beachhead.

D+2:   Units of 5 Marines further liase with 1 Marines to secure southern flank. Enemy armored losses inflicted by MAG.

D+2, noon: Ascom City captured (apart from scattered resistance emitting from the drainage system).

Last light: Kimpo Airfield is captured.

D-Day+3,
0300 hours
to dawn: Fiercer enemy counter-attacks, assisted by T-34 tanks in strength. Pershings called up to secure perimeter of Kimpo.

D+3:   A vanguard of U.S. Army detachment (32 Infantry) lands at Inchon.

D+3: Destroyers become of marginal value, and then useless, as their range is too short to support the inland advancing Marines. The same duly becomes true of the cruisers later that day, but not before HMS *Kenya* had fired over 300 rounds of 6-in. shells on to Hill 123, east of Sosa and north of the road to Seoul.

D-Day+4: 32 Infantry relieve Hawkins' 1/1 Marines and the Marine Reconnaissance Coy in the south beachhead.

D+4: Capt. Fenton (1 Bn, 5 Marine) captures Hill 118 without loss.

D+4,
last light: Maj. Gen. Barr's 7th Division, U.S.A. (with 31 Regt), fully ashore. Almond is anxious to capture Seoul not later than D+10 (September 25th).

D+4,
onwards: Air strikes hit Seoul from Kimpo Airfield. (One MAG Corsair had already landed illicitly at Kimpo from carrier while it was yet out of bounds.)

D-Day+5: 1 Marines' day of hard fighting and great gallantry; early tank battle on ridge west of Yongdungpo. MacArthur and staff tour CP's.

D+5: Murray orders passage of the Han, involving 3/5 Marines (Taplett), 2/1 Marines (Sutter), Houghton's Reconnaissance Coy and swimmers to establish bridgeheads. Attempts fail because of unexpectedly heavy enemy machine gun fire.

D+5,
1000 hours: Second attempt to cross the Han succeeds. Taplett's success is consolidated by the 2/5 Marines (Roise), followed by 2 Bn KMC which occupy the Kumpo Peninsula.

D+5: 7 Marines (a piecemeal unit from every theater of command) reaches Inchon.

D-Day+6,
0630 hours: The main battle for Yongdungpo begins. The NKPA try to resist Puller's 1st Marines.

D+6,
0730 hours: Hawkins (1/1 Marines) thrusts at Yongdungpo from Kimpo. Barrow (A Coy) moves from the hill feature, Paeksok, to the town center and engages the 87th NKPA Regt.; spends two nights in the town, beyond radio contact. Enemy evacuate towards Seoul.

D+6,
1530 hours: Ridge (3/1 Marines) begins to move, supported only by his Weapons Coy, over the Kalchon River into Yongdungpo.

D+6,
1900 hours: Bland (B Coy 1 Bn 1 Marines) draws adjacent with the root of Barrow's thrust. Many wounded Marines evacuated.

D+6,
1930 hours: Maj. Gen. Almond asumes command of X Corps ashore. His command is bedeviled by acrimony between himself and Maj. Gen. Smith (1 Marine Division).

D+6: 32 Infantry, 7 Div., in action for the first time when (2/32 under Lt. Col. Mount) it cuts the Suwon-Anyang corridor.

D+6: NKPA reinforcing their regiment's depleted garrison with 5,000 communists, commanded by the Russian-trained Gen. Wol Ki-chan. The UN surround Seoul, except from the east. Almond deploys Marines, who were to take Seoul alone. Puller and Murray confident that they can hold 10,000 NKPA on the northwestern sector. 7th Infantry consolidating its position in the south.

D+7:   32nd Infantry (Col. C. Beauchamp) captures
          Suwon, despite some confusion as to the identity
          of enemy tanks and the consequent loss of its
          Operations Officer, Col. Hampton.

D+7:   5 Marines placed in line to take An San, the
          mountain from which Wol directs the defense of
          Seoul. Bitter fighting.

D-Day+8: At last light the Marines are still pinned down in
          their foxholes; Wol's hordes sustain Marine fire-
          power, but U.S. land movement restricted. Al-
          mond gets impatient and threatens to break the
          Marine integrity by placing an Army brigade be-
          tween them on the western flank, but relents in
          the face of angry pleading by Gen. O. P. Smith.

D+8:   1 Cavalry Division (spearheaded by 3/7 Cavalry
          under Lt. Col. Lynch) ordered by Walker to
          breakout of the Pusan perimeter. (An unofficial
          breakout had begun on D+1.)

D+8
and 9:   Two distinguished pilots killed in "flak-trap" over
          Seoul: Lt. Col. Lischeid and Maj. Floeck, who had
          demolished many enemy tanks.

D+9:   1 Marines (Puller) cross the Han.

D+10:   1 Marines and its armor finally capture Yong-
          dungpo, and withstand a counter-attack.

D+10:   31 ROK (Seoul) Regiment strikes Hill 348, the
          capital's great southern prominence.

D+11:   Maj. Gen. Barr (7th Infantry Division) is ordered
          by Almond to advance ten miles south from Suwon
          to Osan.

D+11,
0826 hours: The first tenuous link-up between X Corps and
          Eighth Army.

D+12: L Troop, 7th Cavalry, close up and the enemy flee. Of the 70,000 enemy troops in South Korea only 25,000 get away north of the 38th parallel.

D+13,
Sept. 28th: Seoul officially falls to X Corps; enemy pursued on all fronts. UN halts briefly at 38th parallel. MacArthur formally hands back authority to the South Korean Government, in the person of President Syngman Rhee.

OPERATION CHROMITE SUCCEEDS BEYOND EVERYONE'S SECRET FEARS.

The Command Structure for
Operation Chromite

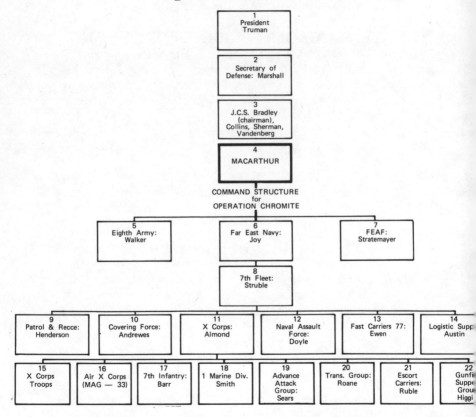

	1 President Truman	
	2 Secretary of Defense: Marshall	
	3 J.C.S. Bradley (chairman), Collins, Sherman, Vandenberg	
	4 MACARTHUR	

COMMAND STRUCTURE
for
OPERATION CHROMITE

5 Eighth Army: Walker	**6** Far East Navy: Joy	**7** FEAF: Stratemayer

8
7th Fleet:
Struble

9 Patrol & Recce: Henderson	**10** Covering Force: Andrewes	**11** X Corps: Almond	**12** Naval Assault Force: Doyle	**13** Fast Carriers 77: Ewen	**14** Logistic Supp Austin

15 X Corps Troops	**16** Air X Corps (MAG — 33)	**17** 7th Infantry: Barr	**18** 1 Marine Div. Smith	**19** Advance Attack Group: Sears	**20** Trans. Group: Roane	**21** Escort Carriers: Ruble	**22** Gunfi Supp Grou Higgi

It is of interest to note that X Corps consisted of 71,339 men, 13,000 of whom were put ashore on D-Day; and JTF-7 of 230 ships (i.e., 7th Fleet involved at Inchon).

N.B.: Smith, and not Almond, commanded operations at Inchon on D-Day.

Problems of an Inchon Bibliography

The British reader faces the double problem of alienation from most works and source material of the Korean War, which was naturally inclined to be an American preserve. The conflict was remote in time and place, fought, as it was, on an almost unknown peninsula on the other side of the world nearly 30 years ago. The war put South Korea on the map as an industrial power, more so than it had been under Japanese rule. Relative to most wars of such importance, there is little in Britain or the United States of bibliographic durability. Even much which the Americans published in the decade following the armistice at Panmunjom is long out of print. Many were ephemeral little works which were not intended to last, either as literature or military history. Gradually, British books suffered the same fate.

Apart from the young and barely comprehending cadre of British national servicemen and the U.S. draft, this was the first time since 1915 that an objective and unprofessional eye was absent *in situ* from a major international conflict. And while the Western Front during World War I produced its poets and pamphleteers on both sides, Korea was altogether too unreal and the enemy too humanly unrecognizable to evoke the sentiments of a European war. Unlike the Spanish Civil War, Korea was too sudden and remote from familiar social cause to attract literary adventurers (even if they had been permitted)—the Hemingways and the Orwells—to take up arms on behalf of the left-wing which was no longer a chance to display a little fashionable belief to one's friends, but was an uncompromising and harsh reality which spelt only treason. Thus no great literature came from the frozen tundra of Korea (the nature of modern warfare, once the first great shock had been experienced, does not encourage it), although American and British journalists sent back some memorable dispatches. No one seems likely to do for Korea what Hugh Thomas did for the Spanish Civil War when he produced his finally comprehensive and monolithic study of that tragic episode in every conceivable cause and effect, although Korea consumed far more American and British lives than its predecessor (the British lost 686 killed in Korea and about 500 in Spain, while the American losses, of course, bear no comparison). Nor is there anything from Korea which combines the literary merit and historical accuracy of Chester Wilmot's *Struggle for Europe*. One of the best narrative accounts to result from the war, at least from the British contingent, was Gen. (then Capt.) Farrar-Hockley's *The Edge of the Sword* (1954); but this dealt only with the experiences of 1 Gloucesters of which the author was then adjutant. Such limitation illustrates the British difficulty at Inchon. Even for Korea as a whole, most people in Britain are completely baffled as to why the war was fought at all and, quite frankly, are not very interested. We should be, for even the process of thought informs.

I believe that the only British work which has any claim to be a comprehensive history of the war is David Rees' *Korea: The Limited War* (1964). Since Britain contributed only a unit of 41 Marine Commando, a few aircraft of the Fleet Air Arm (from H.M.S. *Triumph*) and two light cruisers to *Operation Chromite*, the United Kingdom had to wait for an American book—Robert D. Heinl's *Victory at High Tide*—to be republished under Leo Cooper's imprint in 1972 (published in the U.S.A., 1968). I would not dispute that Colonel Heinl, a retired Marine who served in Korea, used his closer access to Marine Corps records to write a fuller tactical history than I do here. But his book takes little account of the overall strategy, and none of the diplomatic effect which Inchon and its aftermath had on the U.N. alliance, notably between Britain and the United States. To these omissions I have tried to address myself, as the background of the Inchon landing, realizing, of course, that Colonel Heinl's fascinating book could hardly be comprehensive in every respect. A compromise between Heinl's and Rees' accounts of that campaign, suitably rescaled, when Rees was preoccupied with the philosophical problem of limited war and Heinl with the nuts and bolts of the amphibious operation, would have been ideal and a splendid balance.

Portraits of MacArthur, of course (of which, believing that I am up-to-date, I cite the best), abound in the United States; but because many of the General's apologists have been inspired largely by the MacArthur charisma, or have fallen victim to his personality, there has been little inclination to pursue criticism of him into Korea where their hero had assumed the mantle of Caesar only briefly before suffering the fate of Hannibal after Zama. Trumbull Higgins' *Korea and the Fall of MacArthur* is perhaps the most relentless hunt for the truth among the shadows. Gen. Ridgway's book, apart from having the unique authority of a Commander in Chief, assesses MacArthur very objectively under the circumstances of their close relationship. Gen. Ridgway wrote to me on June 25, 1978:

> In my book I portrayed General MacArthur as objectively as I could. My book is still very much in demand and available in book stores here after eleven years, and I have yet to receive anything but praise of it—not one adverse comment on my handling of MacArthur.

I feel sure, from my own study of it, that any reader will feel as pleased as does its author. The book is important because of all the Korean War generals only Ridgway and Maxwell Taylor (the last commander of the Eighth Army–U.N. ground forces), corps and divisional airborne commanders in the notorious *Operation Market Garden* in September 1944, accepted and practiced limited warfare absolutely and without reservation. Ridgway sought, in his book, to answer the questions, "Why are we here?" and "What are we fighting for?" (Appendix 4), with which he had given a sense of purpose to a bewildered and demoralized army following the retreat from the Chongchon. Unfortunately there is not much space devoted to Inchon in General Ridgway's book, which inevitably has so much else to tell of his own period of command. His Appendix 5 recounts the composure with which MacArthur accepted Truman's humiliating summons. Gen. Ridgway was a fine soldier, greatly respected by the British in Korea; but it is alleged that he did not get on with that legendary Anglo-Irishman, his Deputy, Field Marshal Montgomery,* whose nationality, by diplomatic agreement among the allies, ensured that he had to continue playing second fiddle to a succession of American commanders who had been far his junior during the war, and would become increasingly so. It was one instance of the poorer, less nu-

---

* Despite a disclaimer to any such idea which he voiced on page xi of his book.

merically powerful, nation having to swallow its pride—indeed, an extension of the command structure upon which *Operation Overlord* had been built; when the Supreme Commander himself, prior to 1942, had experienced no more searing an enemy than the Mexicans. To this, of course, Gen. Patton was the notable exception; while no living commander had a personal record of command in war to match General MacArthur's. Certainly, if similarity of temperament alienated Ridgway from Montgomery, there was little to choose between their immodesty, as the former's Appendix 9, which quotes verbatim Gen. Marshall's fine opinion of Ridgway's service in Europe and Korea, readily illustrates. The book is dedicated to Marshall. MacArthur, on the other hand, was overbearingly self-assured, but not I think immodest. Ridgway's work is regrettably no longer available in Britain; and so, for most of the works mentioned here, one must visit the Reading Room of the Imperial War Museum or the Library at the School of American Studies at the Senate House, London University, to find them.

The lack of bibliographical material in Britain becomes correspondingly more difficult when advising members of the Inchon campaign itself. Col. Heinl wrote to me on February 23, 1974:

I can readily visualize your problem as to source material. . . . At the risk of sounding immodest, may I suggest that, in conflict with the official histories, you follow VICTORY? I had the advantage of much later production, of sources not yet open even to the official historians when they worked, and the hindsight capability of running down such conflicts. Questions like those surrounding the August 23rd conference,* the bridging of the Han, even of troop strengths and casualties, are some that come to mind in which the official narratives were not quite on the mark.

I had told Col. Heinl that I was considering this book and, with the greatest altruism and generosity of spirit, he wished me well. In all the particulars he mentioned I have heeded his word and relied upon his Inchon casualty statistics, but regrettably his book is also now out of print in Britain. I should emphasize that it is not my purpose pointlessly to duplicate the information which he so valuably provided, since, as I have said, our purposes were not identical.

And so the works devoted solely to the Inchon-Seoul operation

* To which Ridgway makes no reference in the Korean War Calendar at the back of his own book.

are few and inaccessible. They exist only in libraries, and a few fortunate private collections; but the other undermentioned books are also recommended from a plethora of general histories in order to give the reader a rounder picture of the Korean War, while acknowledging the whole time that *Operation Chromite* was its fulcrum:

A: GENERAL MILITARY HISTORY

Appleman, Roy E. *South to the Naktong, North to the Yalu.* Office of the Chief of Military History, Department of the Army, United States Government Printing Office, Washington, 1961. (A volume in the series, *United States Army in the Korean War*).

Cagle, M.C. and Manson, F.A. *The Sea War in Korea.* United States Naval Institute, Annapolis, 1957.

Congressional Record, 1950–54. *Substance of statements made at Wake Island Conference*, compiled by General Bradley. Prepared for the Senate Armed Services and Foreign Relations Committees, U.S.G.P.O., Washington, 1951.

——. *Military Situation in the Far East.* Hearings before the Joint Senate Committee on Armed Services and Foreign Relations. 82nd Congress; 1st Session, U.S.G.P.O., Washington, 1951 (known as "The MacArthur Hearings").

O'Ballance, Edgar. *Korea, 1950–53.* Faber, London, 1969.

Orbis, Philadelphia. *Strategic Surprise in the Korean War.* James E. Dougherty, Fall, 1962.

Rees, David. *Korea: The Limited War.* Macmillan, Macmillan (U.K.), 1964.

Thompson, R.W. *Cry Korea.* Macdonald, London, 1951.

U.S. Naval Institute Proceedings. *Errors of the Korean War*, M.C. Cagle, March, 1958.

Westover, J.G. *Combat Support in Korea.* Combat Forces Press, Washington, 1955. (Capt. Westover took part in *Chromite*, and is referred to on page 118.)

B: BIOGRAPHY AND PERSONAL REMINISCENCES

Attlee, C.R. (Earl Attlee). *A Prime Minister Remembers.* Heinemann, 1961.

Cutforth, R. *Korean Reporter.* Allen Wingate, 1955.
Higgins, Marguerite. *War in Korea.* Lion Books, New York, 1952.
Truman, Harry S. *Memoirs, Vol. II: Years of Trial and Hope.* Hodder & Stoughton, London, 1956.
Ridgway, Matthew B. *The War in Korea.* Barrie & Rockliff, London, 1968 (published U.S.A., 1967, as *The Korean War*).
Wheeler-Bennett, J.W. *King George VI: His Life and Reign.* Macmillan, 1958.

C: MAC ARTHUR BIBLIOGRAPHY

Gunther, J. *The Riddle of MacArthur.* Harper, New York, 1951.
Higgins, T. *Korea and the Fall of MacArthur.* Oxford, 1960.
Hunt, F. *The Untold Story of Douglas MacArthur.* Devon-Adair, New York, 1951.
Kenny, G. *The MacArthur I Know.* Duell, Sloan and Pierce, New York, 1951.
MacArthur, Douglas. *Reminiscences,* McGraw-Hill, New York, 1964.
Manchester, W. *American Caesar: Douglas MacArthur, 1880–1964,* Little, Brown & Co., Boston, 1978.
Willoughby, C., and Chamberlain, J. *MacArthur, 1941–1951.* Heinemann, London, 1956.
Whitney, C. *MacArthur: His Rendezvous with History,* Knopf, New York, 1956.

D: INCHON-SEOUL OPERATION

Heinl, R.D.: *Victory at High Tide.* J.B. Lippincott, Philadelphia, 1968. (Published in Great Britain by Leo Cooper Ltd., 1972.)
Montross, L., and Canzona, N. *U.S. Marine Corps Operations in Korea.* Historical Branch, U.S.M.C. H.Q., U.S.G.P.O., Washington, 1954–1957, (Vol. II: The Inchon-Seoul Operation).

APPENDIX D

Abbreviations

Owing largely to advanced technology and logistics several long and ugly expressions have entered military parlance, particularly in the United States, so that in order to economize on space, the following abbreviations have been used throughout this book:

AD	Douglas Skyraider marine bomber
CINCFE	Commander in Chief, Far East
CINCUNC	Commander in Chief, United Nations Command
CP	Command Post
CPVA	Chinese People's Volunteer Army
FEAF	Far East Air Forces
JCS	Joint Chiefs of Staff
JTF	Joint Task Force (e.g., JTF-7: Joint Task Force of the 7th Fleet)
KMC	Korean Marine Corps
LCM	Landing craft, mechanized
LCVP	Landing craft, vehicle and personnel
LSD	Landing ship, dock
LSMR	Landing ship, medium (rocket)
LST	Landing ship, tank
LVT	Landing vehicle, tracked (amtrac)
MAG	Marine Air Group
NKPA	North Korean People's Army
OP	Observation post (long used by the British)
RCT	Regimental Combat Team
ROK (A)	Republic of Korea (Army)
VMF (followed by a number)	Marine fighting squadron

Notes on the Text

CHAPTER 1

1. *Napoleon* by H.A.L. Fisher, Oxford University Press (Home University Library edition, 1945), page 208.
2. From the statement issued by President Truman at the White House, one o'clock on the morning of April 12, 1951.
3. From Karl von Clausewitz', *Vom Krieg*, page 598.
4. Gen. Omar N. Bradley, addressing the House Armed Services Committee, October 19, 1949; fully reported by *The New York Times* next day. Among Bradley's audience of senior officers from all the services was Col. Robert D. Heinl.
5. Gen. Walton H. Walker's order to the Eighth Army in the immediate aftermath of the fall of Chinju in the southwest of the Pusan perimeter. Thereafter the U.N. Command held its ground, until September 16th, when the first break-out stirred towards Maj.-Gen. Almond's X Corps at Inchon.
6. Conclusions of UNCOK (United Nations Commission on Korea) forwarded to the Secretary-General, Trygve Lie, on Monday, June 26, 1950.
7. Gromyko's complaint to Trygve Lie about the exclusion of Red China from the U.N., about which he had boycotted the Assembly and other agencies; he also held China's seat on a "Kuomintangite." His long note of July 4th referred, *inter alia,* to Britain's ill-fated attempt to assist the Czarist army.
8. House of Commons Debates, 5th Series, Vol. 477, Coll. 485-95.
9. *Ibid.*
10. Rees, David. *Korea: The Limited War.* Macmillan, 1964 page 96.

11. Coad, Brig. B.A. "The Land Campaign in Korea," *Journal of the R.U.S.I.*, February, 1952.
12. Rees, David. *Op. cit.*, page 329*n*.
13. From General Vandenberg's testimony to the MacArthur Hearings. His evidence can be found in *Hearings*, pp. 1378-1402.
14. Bryant, Arthur. *The Turn of the Tide* (Based on the War Diaries of Field Marshal Viscount Alanbrooke). Collins, 1957, page 684.
15. MacArthur came vitriolically to call these bases "the privileged sanctuary of Manchuria." (*Hearings*, page 571.)
16. In a news conference on April 17, 1951 President Truman said that his mind had been firmly decided about Gen. MacArthur when he heard of the General's ultimatum to the Chinese Commander in Chief (Lin-Piao) on March 24th, which should first have been issued as a proposition to the Chiefs of Staff. MacArthur exceeded his responsibility by hinting atomic reprisals against a failure to accord with the U.N.'s terms of surrender. Excessive use of authority to undermine the President's was his prime fault. The President said that Gen. MacArthur's letter to Mr. Marshall, Opposition leader in the House of Representatives, suggesting the use of Chinese nationalists in the Korean War only confirmed the President's established opinion.
17. The transcript, *Substance of Statements made at Wake Island*, is fully reprinted in Revere and Schlesinger, pp. 253-262.
18. From a special communique; MacArthur to U.N., November 28, 1950. Also *Hearings*, p. 1834.
19. Von Clausewitz. *Op. cit.*, page 598.
20. Speech by President Eisenhower from the White House to the American nation, delivered at 10.0 p.m. on July 26, 1953. Seated in a chair which Queen Victoria had presented to the White House the President also said ". . . in this struggle we have seen the United Nations meet the challenge of aggression. . . ."

CHAPTER 2

1. Ridgway, Matthew B. *The War in Korea*. Barrie and Rockliff, 1968. (Published in the U.S.A. as *The Korean War*, 1967.) This quotation is taken from page 33.

2. Willoughby, C., and Chamberlain, J. *MacArthur, 1941–51.* Heinemann, 1956, pages 347-348.
3. This remark was almost exactly echoed by Admiral Doyle's communications officer, Commander Monroe Kelly.
4. Ridgway, Matthew B. *Op. cit.*, page 40.
5. Walker, Walton H. *Ibid.*
6. Ridgway, M. B. *Ibid*, page 38.
7. Doyle was referring particularly to the hydrographic and navigational difficulties. *Vide* Rees' book, page 81.
8. Admiral C. Turner Joy, the Allied Commander-in-Chief, Far Eastern Naval Forces, had his "own misgivings erased" and reported that his service chief, Admiral Sherman, was "almost persuaded" by MacArthur's advocacy. *Vide* Ridgway's book, page 39.
9. This was Harriman's view of *Operation Chromite*, as expressed to Ridgway and Norstad after MacArthur's conference, August 6 to 8, 1950.
10. This was said on July 14th, the day after MacArthur had confirmed that Operation *Bluehearts* was no longer feasible. But Collins still awaited the moment when the Russians, using such devices as Korea to preoccupy the allies, would march on the Rhine.
11. See Heinl, R. D. *Victory at High Tide.* Leo Cooper, London, 1972, page 20. (J. B. Lippincott, Philadelphia, 1968.)
12. MacArthur finished his briefing on August 23rd: ". . . I can almost hear the ticking of the second hand of destiny. We must act now or we shall die. I realize that Inchon is a 5,000 to one gamble, but I am used to taking such odds. . . . We shall land at Inchon and I shall crush them!" See Rees, *ibid.*, page 83 and Heinl, *op. cit.*, page 42.
13. Sherman's remark before he and Collins left for Washington after the conference on August 23rd. But next morning Sherman and Shepherd privately pleaded with MacArthur to land at Posum-Nyon where frogmen would ensure that the beachhead at Inchon could support such an operation. The frogmen affirmed that this was possible. Rees here uses the word "confidence" and Heinl "optimism." I have been unable to confirm which was correct.
14. President Truman's reaction to Averell Harriman's conveying to him Gen. MacArthur's advocacy of the Inchon–Seoul operation. *See* Heinl, page 14.
15. Heinl, *ibid.*, pages 6-7. In keeping with the reduction of all

amphibious, naval and marine strength and material, the Navy had a wartime maximum of 610 landing craft which, in five years, had been reduced to ninety-one. Inchon focused the need of the Chiefs of Staff on the Navy and the Marine Corps.

16. This conversation occurred on June 29, 1950; and Sherman waited for two more worsening days until, after lunch on July 1st, he eventually sent his highly confidential "Blue Flag" to Joy.

CHAPTER 3

1. From the log of Rear Admiral W. G. Andrewes, RN, for September, 1950. Used by Colonel Heinl in his *Victory at High Tide*, on pages 65 and 79.
2. Heinl. *Op. cit.,* page 88. AR, Commander Rocket Division, September 11, 1950 (in Office of Naval History).
3. Heinl. *Ibid.,* page 92.
4. Heinl. *Ibid.,* page 93.
5. Heinl. *Ibid.,* page 93; and see *Notes* (7) on page 278.

CHAPTER 4

1. Marine Corps Historical Branch, interview with Major M. J. Sexton on May 16, 1951.
2. At the end of the Gen. MacArthur's briefing in Tokyo on August 23, 1950.
3. Marguerite Higgins, who wrote this and the extract below for *The Herald Tribune* was the first woman war correspondent to report on major international hostilities outside the Spanish Civil War.

CHAPTER 5

1. Montross, L., and Canzona, N. *U.S. Marine Corps Operations in Korea, Historical Branch,* USMC HQ USGPO, Washington (1954–57) (Volume II: The Inchon–Seoul Operation, page 117.
2. Montross and Canzona. *Ibid.,* page 115.

3. *Ibid.;* and partly quoted by Heinl (*op. cit.*), page 111.
4. SAR, 1st Marines, January 6, 1951 (in Marine Corps Historical Branch), also quoted by Heinl (*ibid.*), page 112.
5. Letter, Major Edwin H. Simmons to CMC, March 28, 1955 (in Marine Corps Historical Branch). The text given here differs, due to some unknown error, in material respects from that ascribed to Major Simmons in the official Marine Corps narrative (page 116), citing the same source.
6. Davis. *Marine!,* page 257.

CHAPTER 6

1. This remark was reported to Colonel Heinl by General Cates.
2. Heinl. *Ibid.,* page 131.
3. I can find no authority for the remarks made in this paragraph, and below it, but they are quoted on pages 131-132 of Colonel Heinl's book, alleging his belief.
4. Winston S. Churchill: The speech to the House of Commons in which he announced the victory of General Montgomery's Eighth Army at El Alamein in November, 1942.

CHAPTER 7

1. AR, USS *Rochester*; ROP, Flag Officer Second-in-Command, Far East, No. 6, March 20, 1951.

CHAPTER 8

1. Carter, Captain Johnny L., letter to CMC, April 19, 1955 (in Marine Corps Historical Branch).
2. Westover, Major George C., undated comments of draft manuscript, *The Inchon-Seoul Operation* (in Marine Corps Historical Branch).
3. Fenton, Captain Francis I., interviewed by Nicholas Canzona for official history, July, 1955.
4. The assault on the ridge is described in Captain Carter's letter of May 31, 1955 in SAR, 1st Tank Battalion; and SAR 1st Marines. WD, USS *Badoeng Strait*, confirms that this air strike was by VMF-323.

5. On the morning of September 19, 1950 Smith and Almond conferred about the first passage of the Han, as a result of which Smith wrote this skeptical log which is in keeping with the reservations which he had of the unfortunate X Corps Commander.
6. These propaganda leaflets, used by the North Koreans on the Army of the Korean Republic, raised morale by their quaint, and rather absurd, English.

CHAPTER 11

1. In view of the Army's failure to recognize the gallantry of the 1st Marine Division, the Navy's Presidential Citation for 1951 was presented to the Marines, although they had been serving under Army orders at Inchon-Seoul.
2. This information from the dispatch was about all that was correct. Otherwise *Pravda* alleged that MacArthur sent British and New Zealanders in first to take the initial fire before committing his own kinsmen. The force consisted of "the most arrant criminals at Inchon, gathered from the ends of the earth. . . ."

Index